*To Hazel & Ian
Many thanks for the lift
Sue Brians*

Percy's Bus

Percy's Bus

Susan Briars

The Book Guild Ltd

First published in Great Britain in 2022 by
The Book Guild Ltd
Unit E2 Airfield Business Park,
Harrison Road, Market Harborough,
Leicestershire LE16 7UL
Tel: 0116 2792299
www.bookguild.co.uk
Email: info@bookguild.co.uk
Twitter: @bookguild

Copyright © 2022 Susan Briars

The right of Susan Briars to be identified as the author of this
work has been asserted by them in accordance with the
Copyright, Design and Patents Act 1988.

All rights reserved. No part of this publication may be
reproduced, transmitted, or stored in a retrieval system, in any form or by any means,
without permission in writing from the publisher, nor be otherwise circulated in
any form of binding or cover other than that in which it is published and without
a similar condition being imposed on the subsequent purchaser.

Typeset in 11pt Minion Pro

Printed and bound in the UK by TJ Books LTD, Padstow, Cornwall

ISBN 978 1914471 452

British Library Cataloguing in Publication Data.
A catalogue record for this book is available from the British Library.

This story is based on the diaries of my father.
(Names have been changed to protect the innocent and the guilty!)

Chapter One
Into Gear

How did I become involved with buses? Simple. Love! Let me explain. I'd been courting Alice for six years and it was time to settle down, but how could we on my tiny wages of twenty-one shillings a week? That was my take-home pay as a chauffeur in 1935 – poor wage even for those times. So, sponsored by Alice's uncle Bill, who worked as a bus mechanic, I borrowed my brother's suit, which was somewhat short in the leg, and hurried over to Leicester from where I lived in Lincoln, to try for a job driving Midland Red buses for a magnificent wage of £3 per week. I got the job and so begins my tale.

The training was very intensive and involved driving a variety of vehicles, bus maintenance and a really difficult driving test. I had been driving limousines as a chauffeur for a number of years but had never taken a test, which was the norm in those days. However, I passed the test with flying colours and, at last, was the proud owner of a Public Service Vehicle Licence, ready to face the terrors of the road.

In July 1935, kitted out in my smart brown uniform with its silver buttons, flat cap with silver and red cap badge, and oh-so-shiny shoes, clutching the somewhat daunting "Book of Rules", I was ready to face the world – well, at least the good people of Leicestershire. But were they ready for me?

The company was run on very efficient lines, being composed of two departments – engineering and traffic. Drivers, mechanics, cleaners, etc., were classed as engineering, whilst conductors, inspectors and office staff made up traffic. The engineering side were "on hire" to traffic, which created a competitive atmosphere and worked very well.

The starting wage was one shilling per hour (5p in today's money), plus a petrol bonus, which would be awarded if you were careful with fuel and could be anything up to six shillings a week. To earn this bonus, the drivers got up to all sorts of tricks, like turning off the engine when not needed for a few minutes, especially when there was a large queue waiting to board.

I've even known drivers turn their engine off so that they could coast downhill. Eventually, this bonus was stopped when one driver was overheard boasting to his mate that he had earned a shilling bonus on his day off!

It was really hard work driving the petrol buses with no power steering – really gut-wrenching. All newcomers were issued with body belts to support the stomach muscles, so no wonder the drivers all ended up with the bus drivers' paunch – pure muscle! Well, that's my excuse and I'm sticking to it!

There was no comfort in the cab either, as the driver's seat consisted of a plywood plank covered in oilskin, fixed above a thirty-five-gallon petrol tank. You could always tell a driver by the shiny seat of his trousers.

It was no wonder that a driver would climb down from his cab at every opportunity to ease his aching backside.

Discipline was very strict and inspectors tried to make sure that the numerous rules in the book were *obeyed*! But "getting away with bending the rules" is my middle name, as you will discover in later chapters. However, an inspector's word was law, and they had the power to fine or sack anyone breaking the rules. But we shall see.

I soon got used to the routine of shift work and made sure I was never late for work, because an infringement of that rule meant you were sent home without pay, and there was always someone to take your place.

A driver was responsible for his bus. Last thing at night, the bus had to be refuelled ready for the next day. Most repairs were done at night, too, and woe betide any garage foreman who had an idle bus on a Saturday, our busiest day.

Saturday night was the worst time, because there was always a queue of buses along the street outside the garage waiting for their turn at the pumps. It was no joke being last man in.

Then before each shift in the morning, we had to spend time checking tyres, wheel nuts, water, etc., and polish the brass handrail and radiator grid, using our own Brasso. Guess what? A dirty bus meant another fine.

It was no use arguing with the inspector – his word was law and he could always charge you with insolence, which meant either docking wages or the sack. Things were harsh but fair. We all got treated the same.

We got used to the discipline and, in a strange way, quite enjoyed the challenges imposed upon us. It was very satisfying to break some petty rule and get away with it. For example, we would sometimes have a crafty smoke whilst waiting for time at a terminus, in spite of the standing order – "No Smoking within the City Boundary" (this included any town or city). The best part was *not* getting caught.

We all worked as a team so the travelling public had a first-class service, second to none. I have actually seen people checking their watches by our buses, which had to run *on time*. There could always be an excuse for running late, but *never* one for running early. If we were running late, the conductor would bang on the rear window of the driver's cab and frantically gesture with his fingers, indicating how many minutes we were behind, not the archer's salute.

As well as checking our bus each morning, we had to be inspected by an inspector. We had to appear smartly dressed, in full uniform, with no missing buttons, white shirt with tie neatly knotted and cap. We also had to carry a box of tools – screwdriver, spanners, pliers, tape, etc., to meet the boss's requirements. "Maintenance begins on the road". There were people called road foremen to see that you did the job properly. What was the mantra? A driver is responsible for his bus. It was definitely hard work, but with the right mates we had some fun and jolly japes.

In the early days, I lodged with some relatives of Alice, my fiancée. They lived in a pretty village called Newtown Linford, a few miles out of Leicester. I used to cycle to work, which was mainly downhill all the way, but returning in the evening, after a day at work, was a real hard slog. It was worse in winter, when I would arrive with frozen hands, feet and face. When I went to bed, it was great to have the in-house tabby cat curled up on the bottom of the bed, keeping my feet warm. The bedroom was not heated, of course, but I was young and fit in those days.

Well, now that I had a good job, Alice and I could get married.

We scraped together £25 for a deposit on a house in Oadby, south of Leicester, and looked at dates for a wedding. Originally, the Saturday before Easter was mooted, but this was the 13th April and in Lent. Alice's family, who were very superstitious and were governed by country lore, could not possibly countenance a wedding on the 13th, and in Lent too, so Easter Monday the 15th April was chosen.

Alice, being an accomplished needle woman, made her own beautiful pink satin gown in the very latest fashion, with a veil to match, which was attached to a circlet of apple blossom made out of wax.

It was "a la mode" in the thirties to wear coloured wedding dresses, and Alice looked stunning. Her younger sisters, who were twins, Rose and Lily, were her bridesmaids, dressed in long gowns of floral crepe, with matching picture hats.

My brother, Alfred was my best man, and I wore my brand-new suit, which I continued to wear for the next thirty years for special occasions. Somehow it shrank in the wardrobe, so Alice gave it to a jumble sale, from whence it appeared on our window cleaner, whose wife paid two shillings for it at the sale.

From left to right: Rose, Alfred (my brother), Me, Alice, Lily

What a picture we all made. This included Alice's big sister Flo. She had married in February on a very foggy day, which prevented them from having photos taken. So she brought her wedding outfit with he, and made use of the family gathering and photographer at our wedding. When she came to put on her going-away outfit, she had the same hat as Alice, but all was not lost – Alice just turned hers around and wore it backwards. It looked fine.

We went on honeymoon to our new house which was situated about three miles from work. As I said before, Leicester is situated in a hollow, so once again it was downhill to work with a slog back up at the end of the day.

We had very little furniture, but it is amazing what you can conjure up with a couple of wooden orange boxes. Alice had been a lady's maid before we were wed and her employers were very generous, supplying us with a beautiful three-piece suite. (This surely showed how highly they regarded her.)

Alice's parents were struggling financially because they had accrued a huge doctor's bill due to her mother being ill for a while and her own illnesses as a child. There was no NHS in those days, so they were paying off sixpence a week. However, they gave us a carving set and a few jars of pickles, jam and honey, which were most welcome.

My folks coughed up some much-needed cash, so we managed. It was hard work, but with a sense of humour like mine, you don't stay down for long, in spite of adversity. Little did we know what was waiting in the wings.

Chapter Two
Blackout Bus

Life was looking good at Christmas 1937. We were settled into our home and were expecting a baby at any time. On 3rd January 1938, our beautiful daughter was born in the local maternity home. She was the first grandchild for both of our parents, so there was great joy all round.

We decided to call her Ann (no e), because it was impossible to shorten. In Alice's home county of Lincolnshire, it was unusual to shorten names, but in Leicester it was very common. So to avoid a shortened name she was baptised Ann, and she was always called Ann, with no second name. So, how come she was called Annie, in later years? Well, that would be a story for a different book.

Everything was going well, but storm clouds were gathering in Europe.

It was exactly twenty-one months after Ann was born that war was declared on Germany. What would life have in store for us now?

At the start of the Second World War, all bus services were cut by fifty per cent, but there were no redundancies, because about the same percentage of staff left to join the forces. I went to volunteer but was told to stay in my job – a reserved occupation.

"Your service will be required for troop movement," was the phrase used, and so it was, much to the relief of my dear wife. The troop movement orders were always at a moment's notice, and we had to act under army orders, as a civilian attached.

I always kept an overnight bag ready for when I got a call. Travelling around was quite difficult at times with the signposts removed and no proper headlights at night, but I never really got lost, thanks to an inbuilt sense of direction.

The most difficult times were driving after dark when the blackout was in force, as the lights on all vehicles were just slits, so we often couldn't see where we were going. One night I drove to Skegness on the coast (HMS *Arthur*) with a bus-load of sailors and a few army personnel, when orders came to stand to. There were five of us bus drivers in the camp, and we had to turn out as well as the troops.

It was organised chaos in the dark, and we stood around in silence waiting for orders. One of my mates took out his pipe and an enormous petrol lighter which he was wont to use and proceeded to light up the whole camp, not just his pipe. Now, I had heard some pretty strong language in the past, but the sergeant major outdid everyone I had heard until then and since. What an education! We did quite a lot of troop movement, such as changing the guard from one airfield to another or to a government property, until the Home Guard took over some of those duties.

Ah, the Home Guard… more about them later.

It was after the battle of El Alamein, when troops were on the move quite a bit, that some paratroopers were billeted in Somerby. One Saturday, I was on the Melton run, via Somerby, with only a thirty-seater bus. We were having to manage with a very depleted fleet of buses. If a bus broke down, there were virtually no spare parts, so we would borrow bits off broken buses to keep the others going – hence such a small bus for such a busy day.

Arriving at Somerby, there were paras going on leave, Land Army girls off home for the weekend and locals going shopping in Melton. There were only two buses a week at this time, so everyone was desperate to get on board. We had a roadside conference, and all agreed to pay when we reached Melton, so on they climbed. How we squeezed over eighty people on a thirty-seater I don't know, but we did, including two people in the luggage compartment. It's a good job the foreman or the police didn't see us that day! (Yes, everyone did pay their fare.)

The blackout was bad enough, and fog sometimes made it even worse, but at least there was not much traffic on the roads. Most people did not own a car, and those who did were limited by strict petrol rationing. A big problem was caused by the American force's vehicles. The Yankee drivers didn't seem to bother much about lighting restrictions or on which side of the road they should be, so if you met one of their wagons at night, it took a while to recover night vision.

I was on a trip one night, groping along in the dark, when an American lorry loaded with GIs going into town overtook me. As they passed by they shone their torches into my face, so I slammed on the brakes until I could see again.

The Yanks I met on my travels were a great bunch of guys – except when driving. They were friendly and courteous, and very generous, often giving me candy for my kids. They were highly amused by the local children who would approach a Yank and say, "Got any gum, chum?" This usually resulted in some sort of candy gift.

One guy even "adopted" my family, and they would send parcels from America from time to time, for several years, even after the war ended, with such things as sweets and beautiful clothing for the girls. Alice used to write to them quite often, but, sadly, as time went by, we lost touch with them, although we remain grateful for such kindness.

In 1942, my wife was expecting our second child when I went down with scarlet fever. Our four-year-old daughter, Ann, had just recovered from it and had had a miserable time in the local fever hospital. We were not allowed any contact for fear of spreading the disease but had to climb up a ladder and wave through the high window, which added to her misery.

She was also very upset that her rag doll and books had to be burned to prevent the spread of infection. The whole house had to be fumigated by the local authorities. I remember the day I fetched her home on the kiddie seat of my bicycle; she sang all the way home.

We think she caught the fever by drinking contaminated water from a fire bucket in the air-raid shelter across the road from our house, which we sometimes used because there was more room than the one we shared with our neighbours and their six children. It was a lot quieter too.

A few days after Ann came home, I went down with the disease, and once again, the house had to be fumigated. I was whisked off to isolation hospital, but there was such an epidemic and a huge shortage of beds that I was put in the children's ward. We were not allowed contact with the outside world but had to communicate through the glass window with signs and notes.

The boy in the next bed would howl like a banshee when he saw his mum at the window. Somehow I managed to get hold of a gobstopper, and next time his mum appeared, I popped it into his mouth to calm him down, and it worked. After that, his mum sent in a small supply of sweets which she managed to acquire, in spite of rationing, so peace reigned.

However, we had a bigger problem than a screaming boy. Because of the isolation, I was not allowed to sign the sick pay papers, so my wife had no money, and the baby was due at any time.

Luckily for us, we had a really good friend, Mrs Tunnicliff, who ran the local tobacconist and sweet shop. She lent Alice enough money so that she could travel with Ann to her parents' house in Lincolnshire, and that was where our second daughter was born, just after the victory at El Alamein, 9th November 1942 – two days after my birthday, which I had to "celebrate" in hospital.

The midwife opened the bedroom window so that my wife could hear the bells ringing for the first time since the beginning of the conflict, as the victory was considered to be a turning point in the war.

The baby was put in a large drawer from the dresser, because there was no cot available. I didn't see the baby until sometime later, but at least I made it to the Christening, where she was named

Susan (black-eyed Susan). She was given a second name – Jane. This was a family name going back several generations.

She was always called Susan, not Sue, and as a child, she insisted on her full name. (It wasn't until she started work that she was called Sue.) Six months later, Susan caught scarlet fever, but because she was not too ill with it, she was allowed to be quarantined at home, as long as we kept quiet about it. We also avoided a third fumigation.

Home Guard

As I was in a reserved occupation during the war, I decided to do my bit by joining the Home Guard. I joined the local troop in Oadby, where I lived.

I was excused parades because of my irregular working hours. As I said before, I could be called at a moment's notice to do troop moving. I was at home when I received an urgent call to report to HQ, which was based in a local pub, the New Inn. It is hardly surprising that many Home Guard HQs were in pubs.

Anyway, I donned my uniform, grabbed my tin hat, gas mask and rifle, and reported for duty. We were ordered to set up a roadblock to check IDs of everyone coming along the road.

There had been a report of parachutes landing a few miles away, so anyone without proper identification was to be detained in the pub until enquiries could be made. A large car pulled up at the roadblock, driven by a chauffeur, and in the back sat the Lord Mayor of Leicester on official business.

The chauffeur produced his ID, but the mayor had left his in his other suit, so we duly escorted a rather irate mayor into the pub. The chauffeur was duly dispatched to collect the mayor's ID, and when he returned, we let the mayor go with a caution. An official complaint was made, but nothing came of it because we were following orders. So that was the day we "arrested" the Lord Mayor of Leicester.

The senior officers in the Home Guard got together and decided that the defence of the realm would be greatly enhanced by sending us on manoeuvres. One was to be at night, and the other, a daylight attack on Melton Mowbray.

The night attack was great fun. We started after the pub closed and everything that followed was blurred chaos. Gerry would have died laughing if he had landed that night.

The daylight attack was more like the real thing, with observers stationed at strategic points. At one place, a platoon hit on the idea of capturing an enemy position by going through an undefended sewerage works. Unfortunately, one of the lads fell into a tank, and after we reluctantly pulled him out, you could smell him miles away. The "enemy" got wind of him before he appeared on the horizon – however, he did get top marks for his unique camouflage!

When I first joined the Home Guard, we were short of equipment, so it was a case of improvisation. We really did use wooden rifles for drills, until the real things arrived. The only time I remember using live ammunition was on the firing range at Kibworth. I was quite a good shot and enjoyed those outings. Usually, though, our rifles were not loaded, unless we were on special guard duty.

During some of my rare time off from work or HG duty, I would go to my allotment. We were all encouraged by the government to "dig for victory", so once again, I did my bit. Now, in those days, I was not much of a gardener, but my wife, who was brought up in the country, was keen, so we grew various vegetables.

My pride and joy were my onions. They were real beauties and would last us weeks, and we could barter with them. Well, one night, enemy aircraft dropped incendiary devices right on my lovely onion bed – they were deep fried in the ground.

Leicester was not devastated like Coventry, but it did receive several attacks. One night, the siren went, and we made our way to the shelter in the garden, which we shared with our neighbours, all eight of them. Fred and I stood watching as the planes went overhead.

He wasn't in the forces, because had a severe back injury and had to wear a steel corset, which meant he could not bend his back.

As we watched, the bombs began to fall. They were obviously aiming at something on the main road a few yards away, but we didn't wait to find out. We dived into the shelter, and Fred literally fell full length on top of me.

One night in the shelter, there was a huge explosion, and it was the only time I was really afraid. I thought our house had been blown up, so it was with great caution and trepidation that Fred and I ventured outside when the all clear sounded.

Everything was OK, and we discovered later that the explosion had been about a mile away. A lucky escape.

Sometimes during a raid we would sit under the iron table in our kitchen; it wasn't as claustrophobic as the shelter. One night, all was quiet and we were asleep in bed when we were woken by a strange clanking sound on the roof.

I jumped out of bed and looked out of the window just in time to see a thick metal cable slide off the roof, trail across the front garden and off up the road. Looking up, I could see a barrage balloon floating along silently in the dawn sky.

I pulled on some clothes and rushed outside to report it, but on my way to the call box I came across an ARP warden, who took the matter in hand. The balloon had escaped from a battery on the local sports ground, and I last saw the blimp drifting off serenely towards Great Glen.

One other event in the shelter was frightening for my daughter, Ann. There was a somewhat smelly Elsan chemical toilet in the shelter, screened from view. She was using the facility when a huge spider started across the floor towards her, and she was so frightened that she climbed up on to the seat to escape but missed her footing and plunged into the toilet. Now, she hated being dirty, and this was the last straw. Everyone else seemed to think that this was funny, but Ann was not amused!

Then came the day I was "bombed" by the Yanks. I was in my bus, driving steadily, in my usual manner, when I met a USAAF lorry, loaded with 500lb bombs (not fused), coming towards me on the wrong side of the road.

I slammed on my brakes and he swerved violently, nearly overturning, and lost three of his bombs, which smashed into the front of my bus. Back at the depot, the gaffer wouldn't believe that I had been bombed by our American allies, but luckily, I had taken the precaution of getting the telephone number of the officer in charge, so the gaffer rang to check and was duly informed that they took full responsibility and would pay for repairs. Hooray!

Bombed – that word conjures up many images and reminds me of one particular night in Coventry.

We had been to Birmingham on a service run and had to return via Coventry, but our route was blocked by an unexploded bomb lodged in a large crater in the middle of the road. A hastily erected sign advised us to divert, but which way? It was difficult enough driving in the dark on familiar roads, but weaving our way around Coventry was almost impossible. My conductor stood leaning out of the door shouting instructions – left here, right here – until a solid brick wall barred the way. Then the sirens went!

It was very frightening, being lost in an unfamiliar city, in the dark, with no-one around (the few passengers had jumped off the bus to seek shelter), and an air raid imminent, but fate stepped in, in the shape of an ARP warden. "What the **** are you doing here?" he shouted. We explained our predicament, and he helped us to escape to the main road, at which point we gave thanks and, foot to the floor, high-tailed it out of there. We could hear the bombs falling in the distance as we drove through Hinckley.

The next day, I had to make a return journey to Coventry, with a bus full of police and workmen. I drove as near to the centre as was possible, to be met by a terrible scene of destruction. The normally jocular workmen, with their ribald wit and coarse laughter, were silent as they filed from the bus armed with picks and shovels.

How could man and muscle sort out this awful mess?

Their first job was to fill in a huge crater which extended right across the road. The tram lines were pointing straight up to the sky at the edge of the hole, and the houses nearby were just heaps of rubble. It was very poignant seeing the remnants of people's lives, like a mangled standard lamp, a piece of curtain, a bath hanging from the wall of what had been someone's home.

I walked around a bit and was surprised by how quiet it was, even though there were lots of people about – they must have all been in terrible shock. I wanted to help but was ordered to take a group of police and workmen back to Birmingham and bring replacements, so off I went.

How could anyone live through such an ordeal?

Chapter Three
Percy's Mates – Conductors Unbecoming

It was during 1941/2 that we began training some of the girls who came to us, under the Direction for Labour scheme, to be conductresses.

A mixed bunch they were too.

I was paired up with a girl who was a mannequin (model), and very beautiful she certainly was. She was not the least bit interested in the job, only in her looks. She was always immaculately dressed, with a full face of makeup, well-manicured nails and not a hair out of place. Even in the uniform she looked stunning and made many a man's head turn to look. But she was useless. I've known a time when the bus was loaded over capacity, as was common during the war, with twenty-four standing passengers downstairs and another twenty standing upstairs, and the conductress demanded a seat, to the amazement of everyone on board. As for taking fares, well, she wouldn't do it if the bus was moving. I'm glad to say that she didn't last long.

As a complete contrast, one girl, Madge, who was rather large, was very useful if there was trouble. One night there were three drunks on the bus causing a bit of a nuisance – well, Madge rang the bell for me to stop. She came round to the cab and asked me to wait a minute. "I've got someone to sort out," she said. By the time I had climbed down from my cab and walked to the rear of the bus, thinking I would have to help, the three men were picking themselves up from the pavement. Madge had slung them off the bus with apparent ease.

It was later that evening that I began to feel a little uneasy. We arrived at an outer terminus in the dark and had to wait quite a few minutes before making the return journey.

I had climbed on to the front of the bus to change the bus number and destination, and big Madge was waiting for me. She lifted me off the step and, as she placed me down very gently, said, "I don't always wear my heart on my sleeve."

Only my quick thinking saved me further embarrassment that night – I scurried off to the gents in the nearby pub and stayed there until it was time to go. Phew!

I have already mentioned the Melton run, and one in particular was one of my favourites – via Knossington. The rural scenery was delightful – real England, and what an escape from the city. One day, I had a very pleasant conductress called June, who was quite pretty and in her early twenties. I had already told her about my youngest daughter, who collected wildflowers. On the outward journey I had seen some forget-me-nots on the edge of a ditch and told June that I would collect a few on the inward trip. We arrived in Melton and waited for the passengers to get on board; amongst them was a young man who'd obviously overheard us discussing the proposed stop to gather the flowers. June offered to get the flowers to save me from having to climb down from my cab, so when we arrived at the spot, June stepped down and began selecting the best specimens, but unbeknown to her, the young man jumped from the bus, quickly and quietly gathered a small posy of the pretty blue flowers, rushed round to the cab, handed me the flowers and returned to his seat on the bus without being seen by June. She never did figure out how I managed to have a bunch of flowers in my hand.

In complete contrast to lovely June was Bert. He was a really pleasant man, but what a face. He had done a lot of boxing in his youth, and it showed. He had a flat nose, cauliflower ears, hard grey eyes and a couple of well-placed scars – a real basher. We certainly had no trouble with passengers whilst he was around.

An ordinance factory was being built in Queniborough, and a fleet of twelve buses was used to ferry the workmen to and from Leicester. The works' siren would go at 5.00pm, and there would be a mad rush to get a seat on a bus. The men would push, shove, elbow, swear and climb over each other to get a seat, generally pushing the conductor under the stairs or completely off the bus in the melee. However, as soon as we heard the siren Bert would station himself on the platform of the rear door, and when they took one look at him, everyone made an orderly line. A good mate was certainly worth their weight in gold.

Joe, a fellow driver, and I were on the miners' run to Desford colliery. We had a bit of friendly rivalry and had a race to see who could get back to base first. On the way back, the road went downhill very steeply, with a humpback bridge at the bottom. This particular day, Joe had really got his foot to the floor, and went over the bridge at top speed. Now, one of his passengers, who worked in the office, was wearing a bowler hat and was sitting on the high bench seat above the wheel arch. When Joe hit the bridge, the poor bloke in the bowler went shooting up from his seat and hit the parcel rack above him with such force that his hat became wedged on his head. It took the strength of two burly miners to release the poor chap. Joe was on the carpet again. Hats seem to have played quite a part in my life, but more of that later.

We amalgamated with a smaller local bus company, who had a fleet of green buses. This stopped the competition for passengers, but we now had the Midland Red Green buses, and the depot was not large enough to garage the extra buses, so a small garage was found on the other side of the city centre. After peak time, nine drivers would take their buses over to the small depot to park overnight, but there was only room for eight. The ninth driver had the job of driving the other drivers back to the main depot.

In those days, there was a small branch line of the LNER, which we passed on our way back. Now, Ernie, one of our drivers, lived a few miles up the line, so he decided to hitch a lift on a slow-moving goods train and hop off near his home.

Next morning, Ernie was missing.

He had jumped on to the train, and it had moved very slowly at first, but once it had negotiated the bend in the track, it had accelerated rapidly, so that it was not safe for Ernie to jump without injuring himself, so he had clung on for dear life until the train finally slowed down going through Nottingham.

Ernie had to hitch a lift home and finally arrived at work about mid-day.

I had one mate, Colin, who did a bit of moonlighting, working for an undertaker. He quite enjoyed the pace of the job and driving the limousines, but he was not really cut out for it.

On one occasion, when he was driving the mourners' car, he noticed a wreath drop from the roof of the hearse, so he got his assistant to jump out of the car, replace the wreath and then return to his place in the second car, whilst the vehicles were still moving, slowly.

Unfortunately, Colin misjudged the lad's speed, and as he approached the vehicle, Colin ran into the poor chap and sent him sprawling on to the pavement, breaking his wrist in the process.

On another occasion, he was reversing the hearse out of the garage when he knocked over an elderly lady who was passing by. He hadn't seen her in his mirror, and the poor lady received a broken wrist too. "We have enough custom without you adding to it," said his boss.

Another time, he dropped his end of a coffin, with the body inside, whilst trying to manoeuvre it through the front door of a house. The family were not amused.

One problem he encountered was not his fault. A very large lady died, and an extra-wide coffin was made to accommodate her. They arrived at the small country church for the funeral, struggled with the bier up the little path to the little church door – only to find that the door was too narrow for such a large coffin. The verger suggested using the rear door, but that was also too narrow, so the service was duly held with the foot of the coffin inside the church, and the head end outside, but there was worse to come. No-one had advised the sexton of the dimensions of the coffin, and as it was lowered with due solemnity into the grave, it got stuck – the grave was too narrow. The undertakers could not apologise enough; they didn't have the nerve to charge the family a fee.

The final straw for Colin was the day he tripped in the cemetery and landed face down on top of a coffin which had just been lowered into the grave. His moonlighting career was buried at that moment.

There was always time for a bit of fun – especially at the expense of others. We had to report for duty half an hour before we were due out of the depot. This time should have been spent preparing the bus for the day ahead, but there was usually quite a bit of horseplay. Two of the lads were especially fond of creeping up on you and tweaking off your tunic buttons or smearing grease or oil on the underside of your steering wheel.

What a mess, with two minutes to off! I eventually got into the habit of wiping the wheel with a handy cloth, or even my handkerchief, much to my wife's displeasure.

One day, a terrible smell was seeping from the engine of my bus. It got worse as the day progressed, so at a terminus, I opened the bonnet to find a half-cooked, rotting fish fastened to the engine block. Revenge had to be planned very carefully. I managed to get everyone in one fell swoop.

Back on the Melton run again. It was market day, and I was presented with a bag of sheep's eyes by the slaughter man's assistant. He roared with laughter as I opened the bag, "Now you can keep an eye on things!" he chortled.

Early next morning, I carefully placed an eyeball on each driver's seat and waited for reactions, with (dare I say it) a sheepish grin on my face. The first driver opened his cab. "What the ****?" he shouted, and gingerly picked up the offending orb and placed it on the bench seat at the back of the bus, ready for his conductor.

Soon there was pandemonium, with shouting, swearing and screaming, from a couple of conductresses. Some of the drivers wouldn't touch the eyes, whilst others began throwing them at each other – there were eyeballs everywhere, until an inspector appeared. It's amazing how quickly the eyes disappeared. I enjoyed every minute.

Talking of market day in Melton, it was quite an eye-opener. Passengers would return to the bus laden with a week's supply of groceries and some livestock. There could be a basket of live chicks cheeping away or a farmer with a live calf in a sack, with just its head sticking out, a hen in a box or rabbits in a bag. The funniest was a buxom, rosy-cheeked lady with a squealing piglet on a string. Both the lady and the pig dropped off to sleep on the way home; they made a lovely picture.

My mate George and I worked out a routine with a pane of glass. We would pretend to carry a huge, imaginary sheet of glass between us, manoeuvring carefully between the parked buses, holding everyone up. The old hands knew the trick, of course, but we caught out the new drivers every time.

In my early days on the buses, trams still ran in Leicester. Now, being a bit of a joker, I decided one day to have a bit of fun with a tram crew, because there was always a bit of friendly rivalry between us.

A tram was stopped at the terminus, in the middle of the road, waiting for the time for it to set off back to town. As I approached from the rear, I saw the conductor going into the nearby gents. Keeping to the nearside lane, I pulled level with the rear entrance of the tram, leaned out of my side window and pressed the bell, which was, for some reason, mounted on the upright post by the entrance, within my reach. Then I continued on my way, and as I passed the front of the tram I saw the driver put down his newspaper and tap out his pipe on the sole of his shoe, then turn the brake release, ready to move off. I pulled up at the next bus stop and watched with great mirth as the tram went rattling by, with its conductor breaking sprint records chasing behind.

We often had unusual items left on our buses, including false teeth, spectacles, a whole Stilton cheese, a fox fur and a white stick, to name but a few. We decided to have a bit of fun with the white stick before we handed it to lost property.

We persuaded George to put on a pair of dark glasses which had been left on a bus and gave him the white stick. He made a great show of pretending to be blind and let a couple of the lads escort him to the driver's cab of his bus. One lad started up the engine for him, and he climbed aboard, groping for his seat and the steering wheel. I have never seen a bus empty so quickly – no way were they going to risk that journey. One lady rushed off to the office to complain that she didn't think it was right to employ blind drivers. The inspector had to reassure everyone it was just a practical joke. There were several of us on report that day. It gave us a laugh at the time and also gave us a valuable lesson – by all means have a joke, but don't get caught!

I found a large meat hook, and as I had a coat with rather long sleeves, I was able to hold the hook in my right hand, without showing my real hand. I walked slowly to my bus, which was already filling up with passengers, and stood at the front so that everyone had a good view of me. I climbed into the cab, making sure I clanged the hook on the steering wheel, scratched my head, then turned and tapped on the rear window of the cab and waved to my conductor with my hook hand. Some of the passengers looked a bit worried, and one or two got up to leave, but to save myself from being reported, I removed the hook, waved to the passengers, most of whom were my regulars and, with a big grin on my face, set off without a hitch. Luckily, most of the passengers enjoyed the joke. However, the people in the office were puzzled by a complaint about a one-handed driver – I wonder who that was?

It was not uncommon when mates were on the same run, one outward and one inward, to wave to each other as we passed. One day I found a top hat, so I wore it on my outward journey and doffed it to the inward driver. Not to be outdone, the other chap found a schoolboy's cap to wear and gave an appropriate salute.

Then, for a couple of weeks we used various forms of headgear – a policeman's helmet, a flying helmet, an ARP tin hat, a deerstalker,

Me in false whiskers

a lady's bonnet and a cardboard crown – until we were seen by an off-duty inspector. On report again. Remember the rule book? Correct uniform must be worn at all times! So it was another fine. All the borrowed hats were returned to their owners, except the top hat, which no-one claimed. I was to have further fun with that.

I had just brought the last bus in one night, and my clippie (conductress) was counting the money and putting it into a tin box to carry it to the office. It was mainly copper coins, threepenny bits and sixpences – lots of them. It took quite a while to tot them up, so whilst she was busy, I climbed down from my cab, very quietly, put on my top hat and a set of white whiskers and beard which I had made out of cotton wool. I tiptoed to the rear of the bus and waited in the shadows. The young clippie gathered her things together, including the box full of money, and stepped off the bus. I moved out of the shadows, and said, in my deepest voice, "I've come for you!" The poor girl threw up her arms, screamed and dropped everything, including the money box, which flew open, spewing coins in all directions. We never did find all of the money, so I had to make up the shortfall from my own pocket – served me right.

I had one conductor who used to drive me mad when he was upstairs, because he would stamp on the floor above my head, to indicate a stop, instead of ringing the bell. Many times I asked him to stop, but he didn't listen, so I decided to teach him a lesson. I watched him go upstairs to collect the fares. Once again came the stamp – that was enough. When he came downstairs, I watched him collect fares, and when he was near the back of the bus, I slammed on my brakes, sending him running the whole length of the aisle and smashing into the front window. He wasn't really hurt, only his pride.

He banged on my side window. "What the **** did you do that for?" he shouted.

"Just a reminder not to stamp on my head," was my reply.

It was bells all the way after that.

We had a small man, Arthur, who came to work as a conductor. He had wanted to be a driver, but his legs were too short to reach the pedals. He had worked for years as a jockey and stable lad, and he could imitate the sound of a horse whinnying. He was my mate on a journey to Billesdon, where we had to wait a while for the right time to leave. Across the road was a milkman's horse-drawn milk float with churns and cans on board. Arthur thought he would entertain the passengers whilst we waited, so when the milkman went into the pub with the day's supply of milk, he let out a loud whinny. Upon hearing this, the horse reared up on his hind legs and then bolted, with milk flying everywhere – what a mess.

The milkman came running and looked as though he was going to kill Arthur, who was really sorry for what had happened. The local bobby was called, and once things had been explained, we were allowed to proceed. I think everyone, except the milkman, found it amusing. Arthur was in trouble when the office found out what he had done.

One of our chaps was nicknamed Gravel. I will explain. He was a bit of a character, and a favourite lark of his was to pick an argument with a policeman. Some took it in good humour, but others, who didn't know him, would mete out some form of punishment. One policeman locked him up in a nearby police box for an hour, and another handcuffed him to the breakdown truck and left him standing there for half an hour. This amused us, as we could really rag him, although it didn't amuse us as much as how he got his nickname.

Our hero was digging in his front garden when he came across a layer of gravel. He thought this would be ideal to make a path in his rear garden, so he kept on digging and loading up his wheelbarrow. The more he dug out, the more trickled down into the hole. Everything was fine until he started to fill his barrow for the third time. There was a sudden crash and the pavement outside his house collapsed, because he had removed most of the gravel which had supported the paving slabs. The council had to come and repair the pavement, and they presented him with a large bill. That was how he gained his nickname – 'Gravel'.

The same lad took a coach-load of people to London on a day trip. He dropped the party in Oxford Street, then proceeded south of the river to park on an old bomb site, which was among several in the area. He parked the coach, then wandered over Westminster Bridge, by the Houses of Parliament, along Whitehall to Trafalgar Square, and found somewhere to have lunch and a cup of tea.

After a stroll along the Embankment, he realised it was time to return to his coach, so back over Westminster Bridge, and it was then he realised he could not remember where he had parked his coach, because all the bomb sites looked the same to him. To make matters worse, his pick-up time was fast approaching, and it was essential to be there on time – he could not fail his passengers. He knew it was on a bomb site, but which one? After a few anxious moments, he enlisted the aid of a passing policeman, who must have thought, *We have a right one here!* The bobby kindly phoned the station, and a car was dispatched to drive Gravel round until he spotted his coach.

Aren't our police wonderful?

As I was driving through a village one day, a young lad ran straight out in front of my bus. I stood on the brakes, stopped the engine and jumped down from my cab in a flash, rushing round to the front of the vehicle expecting to see the worst, but there the lad stood, clinging to my radiator grille, all in one piece, with not a mark on him, looking as deathly white as I felt. My poor conductor came staggering round to the front of the bus, with blood streaming from his nose, which he had banged on a seat as he was pitched forward by my braking hard. We managed to prise the boy's hands from the grille, and I carried him to the grass verge at the side of the road, but he was too shocked to tell us his name. Luckily, a neighbour had seen what had happened and helped us to take him to his home nearby. As soon as he saw his mum, he started bawling his eyes out. The neighbour recounted what she had seen, and the boy's mother gave him a real earful for being so stupid, then turned and thanked me for my quick actions and apologised for her son's action. I think he learned a valuable lesson that day.

Now for a complete contrast.

Earlier, I mentioned some of the strange requests for carrying things on a bus, such chickens, piglets and a coffin – an empty one, of course. Beating all other requests was the man who asked if we could transport his upright *piano* to the next village. Well, I am always up for a challenge, so after a brief discussion with all concerned, we decided that if it could be lifted on to the bus safely, then it could be carried, free of charge.

So, a small group of fit young men, me included, hefted the piano on to the rear platform, and off we went. I drove as smoothly as possible to the next village, where the piano was lifted onto terra firma. To thank us, the owner proceeded to entertain us with a medley of popular tunes. It was the first and last time I was played out of a venue. I must say, I was glad that there was no inspector around, otherwise everything would have been decidedly off-key!

Back to work.

I was cycling to work one morning for the early shift, when I noticed a couple of shop fitters having a cup of tea, sitting on a pile of rubble they had brought out from an old clothes shop they were renovating. I noticed them because it was very early, but mainly because I could see a pair of lady's legs sticking out of the rubble.

I stopped and got off my bike and asked what they intended to do with the plastic legs. They were the sort of model legs used to show off stockings in shops. They said that the legs were being thrown away, but I could have them if I wanted. They must have thought I was a bit mad when I took off my coat and wrapped it around the legs – I was going to have some fun. Thanking the bemused fitters, I pedalled the last couple of minutes to work, with the legs under my arm, tiptoed through the rear entrance and smuggled the legs into my locker before I was seen, then went and clocked in.

That evening, I persuaded Alice to let me have a pair of her old stockings and shoes, ready to have some fun. I went to work extra early the next day, gave the shop fitters a cheery wave and once more used the rear entrance. I retrieved the legs, put the

27

Percy's Bus

stockings and shoes on them, and placed them under the front of one of the buses, with just enough of the legs showing to make them look very realistic in the dimly lit garage. Then I withdrew to watch the reactions. I did not have to wait long for George to arrive – he was usually one of the first in. He started to walk round his bus doing his inspection when he came to the front and saw the legs. "B***** h***!" he shouted. "Help!" I was first to arrive on the scene, of course, and knowing me and my practical jokes, the penny dropped. At first he was a bit annoyed at being tricked with such a scare, but he soon lightened up when we played the same trick on other drivers.

I had endless fun with the legs, especially when going to dances. On a couple of occasions I rigged up a third leg, just like Jake the Peg, diddle diddle dum! I was driving home one evening, with the legs propped up against the rear side window, when I was flagged down by a police car. They thought someone was not sitting properly in the back seat and might get hurt. (This was before seat belts were made compulsory.) They looked in the back of the car and had a good laugh when they saw the false legs. It certainly brightened up their shift, and no doubt they amused colleagues back at the station. I expect they got some ribbing. Well, they didn't have a leg to stand on, or perhaps they felt that they should leg it before the next leg of the inquiry was started.

Enough of this banter, or we'll be legless with laughter, or tears!

Percy Tipsy Turvy

There were strict rules regarding drinking and driving. Any driver found drinking alcohol was dismissed instantly, and if you were found on licensed premises, there was a seven-day suspension without pay, even if you were only drinking tea.

Spot checks were made by flying checkers. These were inspectors or road foremen, who used to travel round in cars to check if you were on time travelling through the villages, and they would also check the pubs. We often used to pop into a pub for a cuppa, and the locals were very good at giving warnings so that we could escape through the back door, or the toilet window, or via the cellar, which was something of a climb. Once I was almost caught, but a friendly customer handed me his coat and hat, and with the brim pulled right down, I managed to walk right past the inspector, wishing him "goodbye" on the way out. I hurried back to the bus to find a few early passengers ready and seated, and the conductor busy eating an ice cream.

He had been to the village shop and had seen the inspector heading into the pub but had had no chance to warn me. He'd watched with great relief when he saw me take off the hat and coat, hanging them on a nearby fence by arrangement with the customer to whom they belonged. Why the inspector didn't inspect the bus first I shall never know, but by the time he emerged from the pub, we were a picture of innocence, and, what is more, we left on time!

We had a few spectacular crashes due to drink. One chap finished up in a rhubarb field. He'd been in a pub and was trying to make up time, then took a bend too quickly – hey presto – rhubarb crumble! Another driver managed to swerve his bus into a ditch, where it balanced precariously at an angle of forty-five degrees, until the rescue truck came and winched it to safety. No-one was hurt, thank goodness. Also, for some reason unknown to me, nobody was sacked.

The worst incident, from the rescuer's point of view, was the driver who skidded into a farmyard and came to a full stop in a huge steaming pile of very ripe manure. Phew, what a smell! Luckily for him there were no breathalysers in those days. Once again, there were no injuries, except for a few bruises for the passengers and the driver's pride. He had to put up with merciless ribbing from everyone at the garage.

It wasn't just drivers who went into pubs. One conductor always carried a small parcel wrapped in brown paper and tied up with string. There was nothing in it, but it gave him a reason for going into a pub, because in those days, village parcel agents were often the local publican, so even if he was seen going in a pub, he had an excuse. I told you that there were ways to beat the rule book.

One Christmas Eve, I was on the last run to Uppingham, via the villages. All the passengers were in a happy mood as they boarded the bus with armfuls of bags, turkeys, holly, mistletoe, etc. My conductor got quite a few kisses that night, and not just from the ladies! By the time we had left the city, everyone was singing carols. The first stop we made was outside a pub, and as the passenger for that stop prepared to step off the bus, he shouted, "The drinks are on me," so everyone piled off the bus and trouped inside the pub. "Come on, you two," he shouted to me and the conductor, so in we went. Just a quick one all round, and off we went again.

The journey continued with everyone singing heartily. Each time we stopped in a village, the process was repeated, until we reached Uppingham rather late, but nobody seemed to mind. (Why is it that village bus stops are usually outside pubs?) There was only one passenger for the return to Leicester, and he was in no fit state to complain about being late. He laid himself out on the back seat and slept the whole journey. I don't remember the journey back to the depot, but we must have arrived in one piece. The conductor said that he had vague recollections of helping me to get the drunken passenger off the bus, and somehow we refuelled, and he handed in the takings. The only thing I can remember is waking up at about four o'clock on Christmas morning in the local playing field, very cold, with a couple of dead rabbits tied to the handlebars of my bike. I had no idea from whence they came. I will add, that was the last time I ever drove after drinking alcohol.

Oh, the follies of youth!

Percy's Mates – Conductors Unbecoming

Me larking about as usual

Chapter Four
Bus on Ice

Winter was always a trying time when we had the closed cabin buses with no heating. There were big holes in the floor of the cab to accommodate the clutch, brake and accelerator pedals, and how the wind whistled through! I found that newspaper was very good insulation against the cold, especially when it was wrapped round the legs and stuffed into one's socks. Also, a sheet or two tucked under your jersey added to your comfort, as did the carefully folded wad that was stuffed into the gap in the sliding window. When it turned really cold, a pair of flannelette pyjamas worn under the uniform was effective, although somewhat bulky and a bit of a nuisance for toilet stops, which were needed after drinking lots of hot tea to keep out the cold.

Some winters were not too bad, but on really cold, frosty mornings, the drivers would arrive about 5.30am, to prepare for the first run. The depot resounded to the sound of men calling, "Gee us a choke!" or "Gizz a pull!". This meant that five or six men were about to hand-crank the engines. A sturdy rope, with a loop on one end, was attached to the starting handle, with one man holding it in position, and the others pulled. One other man would lean over the front mudguard to manipulate the carburettor, with one hand over the air intake and the other on the throttle control. If he didn't get it right first time, he was always reminded about his parentage in no uncertain terms of endearment! Frequently, the language turned the cold air blue – quite an education for a young chap like me, but actions speak louder than words. We had one driver who would kick the hell out of his front wheel if his bus wouldn't start, until the day he miskicked and broke his toe on the hub. At the other extreme, we had one very large, beefy driver who laughed at our pathetic efforts. He'd place one massive hand on the radiator, grasp the starting handle with the other and give it a spin – no problem!

Once we had the engines started, we left them running to warm up, whilst we popped into the canteen for a well-earned breakfast, then out into the cold. The company's motto was, "Every effort will be made to maintain the service!" What lengths we went to, to try and do just that. It was a rule, when there was snow about, to carry a long-handled shovel and a bucket of cinders from the old coke boiler in the office. I have spent many an hour trying to reach my destination, scattering cinders and digging, sometimes winning through but often failing. We had one crew that went missing for almost a week when they were snowed in but were very happy being looked after by a very genial landlord of a village pub.

One time, up in high Leicestershire, there was a lot of snow, more like Siberia that day, and I had been on the Melton run, via the villages, but found the road ahead blocked by a huge drift and had no way to retreat. I left the bus, with the engine running, to prevent it from freezing up, as it was bitterly cold, and, after reassuring the passengers and conductor that all would be well, trudged and slithered half a mile back down the road to a farm to use their telephone to call the depot. Amazingly, the phone line was working, so I rang for fuel and assistance. The farmer and his wife invited us all into their home to warm up, so I struggled back to the bus to collect everyone. I turned off the engine and helped the passengers to the farmhouse, where a blazing log fire and hot drink soon made us all jolly and warm. It was three hours later that the farm dogs, barking in the twilight, warned us of approaching visitors.

The rescue squad from the depot had arrived, looking like an Antarctic expedition. They were muffled up to the eyebrows and were pulling a sledge on which were large cans of fuel and several shovels, stout ropes and lamps. They looked a sorry sight but soon cheered up after a couple of doses of homemade punch!

With the farmer's help they rigged up a makeshift snow plough on his tractor, and he cleared enough of the road behind me, whence the rescue party had come, to enable me to return, if I could just manage to manoeuvre the bus. With a lot of slithering, shovelling, scattering cinders, cursing, sweating and pulling by the tractor, I managed to reverse the bus into the farmyard, so I could then drive back to the depot by a different route. We finally pulled into the garage sometime after midnight!

Later the same week, it was my chance to help another driver, as part of a rescue squad. He had tried to ram his way through a huge snowdrift but had become stuck fast. I drove the bus with the rescue crew, and we were faced with a mammoth task of shovelling tons of snow before the bus could be moved. However, as usual, some bright spark had an even brighter idea, and, thankfully, that bright spark was not me. To save us hours of digging, my mate and I were told to place a large iron bar across the rear seats of the bus, at floor level, and open the rear emergency exit door, through which would be passed a heavy-duty chain. This was attached to the iron bar at one end and the towing vehicle at the other. My mate and I stood well clear, as we guessed what might happen, but who were we to argue? The towing vehicle revved up its mighty engine and began to pull. The chain went taut, we held our breath, then, with an almighty crash, the rear seats of the bus came sailing through the air and crashed into the front of the towing vehicle, smashing the headlights. Isn't it strange how catastrophes and accidents seem to happen in slow motion? Our laughter was short-lived when we realised we would have to resort to the tried and tested method of shovelling tons of snow by hand. There was the usual row back at the depot and a tea-break talking point for us lads for a few weeks.

Now, the bright spark whose idea had backfired had quite a bad stammer when he was agitated, and so did the gaffer, so these two had a blazing row for about twenty minutes, without actually saying much at all.

We had some rough times with the snow and the old petrol buses, but in the evening peak hour, when the factories turned out, every bus would be out of the depot, never mind the weather. One evening, ten or eleven buses had left the depot, at different times, for the journey to Coalville, but by the time they reached the first hill out of the city, there was quite a convoy trying to make headway on the ice up the hill. It had snowed earlier in the day, then it had rained, and a sudden drop in temperature had caused a very sharp frost, so the roads were like shining glass. There was a prolonged struggle for us all to get up the hill, but working together with shovels, cinders or grit, we finally made it. However, we were held up at the top of the hill by oncoming traffic. I was last in the queue, and as a precaution, had steered my nearside wheels onto the grass verge, to give the tyres some purchase, when there was a terrific bang, and my bus shook with the impact of a large lorry hitting my rear corner, ripping off a chunk of bodywork. The lorry driver explained that, on seeing the buses struggling up the hill, he had decided on a different approach.

He had made a relatively fast approach to the hill and had made a fair ascent without stopping. However, on reaching the top, he found that he could not stop anyway, so crunch! By the time we had exchanged particulars, the vehicles in front had moved on again, only to be held up at the bottom of the next hill. So, there I was, sitting in my cab, waiting for my turn to struggle up the next hill, when – crash – it happened again. I climbed down from my cab and found the same lorry embedded in the rear of my bus – driverless! Before the lorry driver had had time to get back in his cab, it had started sliding down the hill, picking up speed as it went along. The poor driver came down most of the hill on his backside. It was the only time I was hit twice by the same vehicle in the space of half an hour.

A brand-new double-decker bus was on a run one very cold evening, when it hit a sheet of black ice on the road and skidded into a ditch. I was one of the rescue squad, which included the gaffer, a couple of other drivers, a mechanic and a young lad who had only just joined the company as a trainee mechanic and who was very keen to please. We arrived at the scene to find the bus in good shape but tilting at a rather alarming angle in the ditch. We prepared the towing equipment, and the gaffer shouted, "Be careful, don't break the windows!" Now, as I mentioned previously, the gaffer had a bad stammer, and the young lad at the other end of the bus obviously did not hear all of the gaffer's stuttering instruction, just "...break the windows!" So, quick as lightning, the lad grabbed a huge spanner from the breakdown truck and ran round the bus, smashing windows with gusto. The gaffer stood with his speechless mouth opening and closing, with his face turning red, then purple, then ash-grey! I managed to grab the lad as he headed for the front windscreen. The poor lad sobbed his socks off when we told him what the gaffer had really said. Needless to say, the lad was teased mercilessly for years, but at least he didn't get the sack and, eventually, he turned out to be a very good mechanic.

Winter may have brought trouble for us drivers, but I also remember the fun times too. Many is the time, in high Leicestershire, I have stopped the bus briefly to enjoy a fantastic snow landscape, with drifts blown into weird alien shapes by the biting wind.

There were happy times too, when I took my two daughters out with a homemade sledge, and we would have hours of fun trudging up the hill and come flying down screaming and laughing as we ended up in a heap at the bottom. We would then drag ourselves home wet, tired and ready for a steaming mug of Bovril. When I was a lad, my brothers and I used Mother's old tin tray as a sledge, which was great fun, until the day I hit a fence at the bottom of the hill and had to trail my bloody nose home, leaving a scarlet track across the snow.

My first winter in employment as a chauffeur, I bought myself a pair of ice skates. The Brayford pool in Lincoln frequently froze over, so we took a chance, on these occasions, to skate by the headlights of cars parked around the edge. Living in Lincolnshire, we would occasionally get over to the Fens to skate on the frozen dykes. Being young and invincible (or stupid), I never realised the dangers, until the day I saw a man go under the ice as it cracked beneath his weight and he did not re-appear until weeks later when his body was found by a sluice gate.

The winter of 1947 was particularly harsh, and coal was in short supply, so any extra fuel was welcome, especially if it was free. I often stopped my bus to pick up a branch fallen by the roadside or gather large twigs whilst waiting at a stop to make up time. My conductor, with whom I shared the bounty, helped too, by hiding the wood in the luggage compartment so that should an inspector board the bus, he would think it belonged to a passenger. It was often quite a job smuggling the wood out of the garage, but we would take it in turns to act as a diversion. The next difficulty was getting the wood home on the back of a bicycle, but somehow we managed, for where there's a will…

I cannot write about winter without mentioning Christmas. I was brought up in a fairly conventional Edwardian household, where children were sometimes seen but never heard! The exception was Christmas. The whole family gathered – aunts, uncles and very Victorian grandparents. We all attended morning service, decked out in our best clothes, dark blue sailor suit for me (not the awful scratchy, starched, white one I was forced to wear in the summer) and fur coats for the ladies, or at least a fox fur round the shoulders, and some outlandish hats.

After church, at home, there were hot drinks and a cold collation with pickled onions as big as eyeballs and pickled walnuts – perhaps (more about pickled walnuts later). Then we would gather round the tree for presents. Simple things, but oh, what pleasure. Maybe a wooden aeroplane or boat, a hand-knitted pair of socks or gloves, usually black or grey, a book, a pencil, an apple, orange, a few nuts and sweets, and a sixpence from grandfather. Such treasures for a small boy! After all this excitement, my brothers and I would have to spend the afternoon quietly reading, drawing or joining in the parlour games. Even Grandfather joined in charades – more about him later, too.

About six o'clock, the adults went up to their rooms to change for dinner. I was made to wash my face and hands but still retained my sailor suit. My father would stoke the fire before he changed, and the table was prepared by Mother and Aunt Eva, ready for dinner. My brothers and I waited eagerly for the dinner bell. The candles on the table were lit by Father just before we all sat down, and how the silver and glasses sparkled. It was so exciting for a young lad like me. What banquets we had for Christmas, and how my mother and aunty had slaved in the kitchen!

We boys had to be silent at the table, unless spoken to by an adult, and we had to sit bolt-upright, otherwise Grandfather would threaten to stick the poker down the back of our shirt to keep us straight. We also had to sit still and eat daintily. Luckily, for me, my parents had fabric covers on the dining chairs, unlike my grandparents, whose chairs were stuffed with horsehair, which pricked my legs terribly when I was in short trousers. This made me fidget, which annoyed Grandfather, and he would make me leave the table, missing out on dinner.

We donned party hats, and the goose or beef was brought to the table, and father sharpened the carving knife with vigour before very neatly slicing the beautifully cooked meat. It was never turkey! So the meal began.

After dinner, we would retire to the withdrawing room, where we would crack nuts and jokes in front of the blazing fire. Grandfather would tell us tales from his youth, then when the kitchen had been cleared, we would gather round the piano for carol singing, until supper time, then off to bed, where I would lay in the dark listening to the sounds of laughter punctuating the quiet, as the adults downstairs played cards.

It seems a little sad that Christmas seems to change with the passing years. When I worked as a chauffeur, I remember having to dress in my best uniform on Christmas Eve, for the presentation of Christmas boxes. We usually received a week's wage as a bonus, if we were long-serving members of staff, or half if we were newcomers. We always had a bit of a party downstairs, a jug of mulled ale and a cold supper put together by the cook, then off to midnight service. I was a server in church by this time and would help the priest during communion. It is the custom in the Anglican church for the priest to drink any wine left in the chalice at the end of mass, and it is usual for the priest to water the wine, but not Fr Joseph.

On Christmas morning, he would celebrate mass at 7am, 8am, 9am, 10am and 11am, drinking the wine at the end of each service, so by mid-day he would be swaying visibly. The two servers had the task of supporting him each side and escorting him back to the vestry. How we negotiated the chancel steps I shall never know – perhaps there was divine intervention!

My Christmases didn't change much until I had my own children – two girls. I worked plenty of overtime in the autumn, to make sure that we could buy a few extras, and it was worth it. I spent hours in my garden shed making doll's houses, furniture, cots, wheelbarrows, go-carts, a sledge, ladder, farm set, and even a bow and arrow for my youngest. My wife would be equally busy with her sewing machine, after the girls had gone to bed, making dresses, dolls' clothes, hair ribbons (which were in short supply after the war) or knitting scarves, hats and mittens. I always tried to finish early on Christmas Eve, because it was then that we decorated the house, never before. We made our own decorations out of salvaged paper or fabric. If I was late, the girls would be resting in bed until it was time to go to midnight service. After church, it was home for a hot milk and honey, then off to bed for two very excited girls, equipped with torches for use when opening presents before it got light on Christmas morning. It was much more exciting than turning on the bedroom light. Somehow, we always managed to fill a stocking and a small pillowcase for them, in spite of being hard up.

One year we bought them both a second-hand bike each, which were hidden in a neighbour's shed until Christmas Eve. I smuggled them into the living room and attached a string to each bike, and laid a trail round the house, tiptoed into the girls' room and attached the end to their stockings at the foot of their beds. We were woken very early that year by the sound of bike bells in the dark. They had followed the string trail all round the house, even in our room, without waking us. I spent most of the morning watching two very excited girls pedalling furiously up and down the road until it was time for capon and trimmings.

Chapter Five
Coughs and Colds – Percy's Life

Talking of coughs and colds reminds me of when I was a lad. I'd had a bit of a cold which had left me with a cough. Now my mother was a great believer in patent medicines, potions and pills, so cough linctus was bought, which was sweet and delicious, and had to be taken as one spoonful three times a day. Now, I'd always had a sweet tooth, so when no-one was about, I sneaked into the bathroom, locked the door, fetched the bottle down from the shelf and swigged the lot! A warm glow engulfed me as I waited for the coast to clear, as I could hear movement on the landing. The bathroom began to revolve, and I remember hanging on to the wash basin, but this came away from the wall, and as I sank to the floor, I have a vague memory of seeing the basin arc over on its lead pipe and, in slow motion, join me on the floor.

My brother, Alfred, was given the task of climbing up a ladder to the bathroom window. He could see me laid out on the floor, so he squeezed himself through the half-open window to unlock the bathroom door. I woke up in bed the next morning, none the worse for my escapade. It wasn't the last time my brother came to my rescue, as you will soon find out.

I frequently had coughs and sore throats, so it was decided that I should have my tonsils removed. In those days, the 1920s, this operation was often performed at home. My mother scrubbed the kitchen table with carbolic soap, the doctor arrived and everything was ready. I can still smell that ether mask to this day. How medicine has improved since then. Anyway, I lived to tell the tale.

I only remember having one cough after the tonsils were removed, and that was shortly after I started on the buses. I picked up a cold which developed into a real hacking cough. It kept me awake at night, and left me tired and sore. I tried numerous potions, but nothing would touch it, not even the "jallop" my brother Jim concocted in his chemist shop. I was really fed up, but luck was on my side again.

One of my conductors, who had worked as a groom, suggested that I take some Pure Terry Beer, which is what was used to treat horses, but I didn't know this at the time. My mate managed to get hold of a bottle, and, when I got home, I had a good swig – not just a spoonful. Well, it very nearly took the top of my head off, it was so strong, and it left me gasping for air for a while, but I haven't coughed since.

In 1948, my wife was very ill with jaundice (hepatitis) and spent at least six weeks in bed. Nowadays she would have been admitted to hospital, but not in those days. I still had to work, because there were not the benefits which are available today. Family, friends and neighbours were wonderful, helping with cooking, shopping, washing and childcare. Alice's best friend, also called Alice, came over every day after work (which meant catching two buses) to make sure the girls were OK. She stayed until I got home from work. My boss was very helpful, keeping me on day shifts. What a marvellous friend Alice was. The girls were six and eleven, and were very helpful doing some of the everyday chores. When I had the chance, I used to do a bit of cooking. My mother was ahead of her time by insisting that me and my brothers learned the basics of cooking. My favourite pudding was rice pudding, nice and sweet. Now, at this time, sugar was still on ration, after the war, so Alice had been very frugal using our weekly ration. Any sugar left over each week was put into the sugar jar, which was used for special occasions.

I was known for having a sweet tooth and really enjoyed the rice puddings I made, delving into the sugar jar, until the day came when there was no sugar left. I mentioned to Alice that we had run out of sugar, so she told me to use what was in the sugar jar. Oh no, I had used up every grain. The sugar jar was empty! I dare not tell Alice, whilst she was so poorly. I can tell you now, a cup of tea does not taste very good sweetened with honey or jam.

Forward a few years to when I was in my fifties, when Alfred came to my rescue again. Hooray for big brothers. I began to be plagued by lumbago, which made certain movements very painful. However, I was alright sitting, and driving, although uncomfortable, I could stand it. I was on a Welsh tour, and my brother Alfred and his wife Jessie were two of my passengers. Halfway through the tour, I was struck down by lumbago, and even with painkillers, I was in agony most of the time. I was alright lying on the bed or sitting and driving, but a simple task like putting on socks was excruciating. This is when Alf came into his own. Every night and morning he came to my room and helped me to dress and undress.

Back home, I was persuaded to go to an osteopath – what a relief! I went into my appointment as an old man, hobbling with a stick, and came out feeling twenty years younger, with a spring in my step. Although throughout the years I suffered from time to time with a bad back, but never such a painful one that I had in Wales. I have kept fairly well since.

I am reminded of my youth when I noticed that I couldn't see what was written on the blackboard at school. I was about twelve at the time, and nobody would believe me when I said I couldn't see. Perhaps people thought I was making up stories, but not this time. Nobody in the family had spectacles, except to read with, and mother never admitted to needing glasses, although it was quite clear she had difficulty reading. My schoolwork began to suffer, and I failed the end-of-year exams, because I had missed so much, being short-sighted. To make matters worse, I was made to stay down a year to catch up. The family thought I was a bit thick, but I just could not see clearly. Things finally got sorted on a trip into the country. My father pointed out a rabbit in the field – what rabbit? It was evidently in plain sight, but I couldn't distinguish it from its surroundings. The next day I was taken to have my eyes tested – I was short-sighted and needed glasses. How my world changed. I could now see!

Travel forward in time to my own children. My daughter Ann, when she was young, had great difficulty swallowing and so did not like solid food. She would drink any amount of liquid, but that was not enough to feed her properly, so she was quite underweight for her age. The doctor suggested giving her cocoa made with cabbage water to give her extra minerals, but as a last resort, suggested that she should have her tonsils out, as they appeared enlarged. A date was fixed for the operation, and afterwards the doctors agreed that she should go to the convalescent home in Charnwood Forest, for two weeks to, and I quote a doctor, "build her up a bit". After one week we were able to visit, and poor Ann, she had been bullied by a much older girl, and she was very upset. Alice and I took immediate action. Alice went with Ann to collect her things, and I went to see Matron. Now, I am usually a quiet, calm person, but Matron's attitude alarmed me. When she said I should give Ann a good smack for playing up, like she had done, and it was the only way to quieten an hysterical child, I saw red. Nobody hits my children (I am a Scorpio and will fight to the death for my children). By now, Alice reappeared with little Ann, who cowered behind her on seeing the matron. We scurried out of the building and caught the next bus home. As a treat for Ann, to cheer her up, the following weekend we went to Lincoln to visit family. We were at Alice's parents' home, and Ann was still not cooperating with eating – she did not yet have the right eating habit. We put her dinner in front of her and were pleased to see her digging her fork into the mashed potato and eating a small mouthful – but that was it. No use fussing about it. Alice's mother scraped the food into the dog's bowl. We all finished our meal, and I went out into the garden with Ann to play. After a while, we came in and Ann went to the dog bowl, sat down and began to eat her dinner. Alice was horrified to think Ann was eating out of the dog's bowl and was going to stop her, but her mother held her back. "Let her be," she said, "it's a clean bowl." From that day onwards, Ann thrived and never again had a problem with food. So if you have a child who won't eat, try serving their food in a dog's bowl – a right good dog's dinner!

(Only joking – or am I?)

The next operation was Susan's a few years later. She needed her tonsils removing because she was plagued with tonsillitis, so she had to go to the Nissan hut clinic in Leicester. These are her words:

"I was only four years old, but I have a clear memory of the event. Mum and I travelled on the bus to the clinic on Clarendon Park Road. On arrival, I had to change into my pyjamas and stow my few belongings in my bedside cupboard. Then Mum had to leave, but before she went, she gave me a colouring book and a pack of crayons to keep me occupied. I loved colouring and could do it properly – just like my big sister Ann showed me, no going over the lines. At the end of the room there was a cupboard with various toys, games and puzzles to keep us busy. Some of our time was spent looking out of the window watching the red squirrels jumping from tree to tree – a real acrobatic show!

"The next morning was the operation. I remember walking into the operating room, where I was lifted on to the bed. There were several adults in the room with masks on their faces. There was a huge light hanging above the bed. One of the doctors, who was not wearing a mask, explained what he was going to do, and asked if I could count to ten. Of course I could count to ten – I could even count to a hundred! He put the rubber mask on my face and I began to count – one… two… three… four… five… six…

"The next thing I remember was waking up in bed with a sore throat. There was a nurse sitting beside my bed, who offered me a sip of water. After a while, the girl in the next bed began to wake up, and, before the nurse could stop her, she poked her fingers down her sore throat, causing a haemorrhage. Blood started pouring out of her mouth, so the nurse grabbed a towel to catch the flow and turned to me and said, "Keep an eye on her whilst I get help." I sat on my bed staring for all I was worth at the girl in the next bed, whose white towel was turning red. What else could I do? I was only four! Help arrived rapidly. She was lifted on to a trolley and rushed out of the ward. I'm glad to say, she returned some time later, still sleeping, but with a nurse in attendance.

"When she woke up later, I offered her my colouring book, to cheer her up. The picture she chose to 'colour' was of a kitten playing with a ball of wool. Horror of horrors – she did not know how to colour properly; she just scribbled all over the page with a green crayon. She was five years old and couldn't colour! I was very upset because she had ruined my lovely colouring book. Mum cut the offending page out of the book when I got home. One other thing I remember was the jelly and ice cream we were given to eat. Jelly – mmmmmm!"

Back to me – I love jelly too.

The mention of blood earlier, reminds me of the time at work when there was a drive to recruit more blood donors. I decided it was something I could do, so I turned up at the next session. When the staff discovered that I was O rhesus negative, they were thrilled, because my type of blood could be given to anyone but only negative could be given to me. Evidently, only about thirteen per cent of the world population have rhesus negative blood – that makes us very useful and quite rare. Over the years I have given blood regularly, which totalled over fifty sessions, and have the medal to prove it. Alice was also rhesus negative but could not be a donor because she had had hepatitis; also, there was another problem. At the sight of blood, Alice tended to faint. It seems strange, when her three sisters were nurses, that she had this fear of blood and hospitals.

Enough of illness. The next chapter is much lighter, with not a cough or sneeze to be heard. Bless you!

Chapter Six
Percy Coach and Horses

After all the ups and downs of the war years, everything began to settle into a normal routine once more, except that I was promoted to the elite bunch of drivers known as coachmen. I was issued with a coveted white coat and cap cover, which we always wore when driving coach trips. When I was not on coach duty, I did my normal service driving. The excursions took me all over the country – seaside, stately homes, London sights, theatres, races, etc. Some would say it was an easy life, but it often meant long hours and some awkward moments.

One beautiful day, I took a party of twelve gentlemen and ten ladies to the motor racing at Silverstone. Everything went well until a freak thunderstorm stopped the race and soaked the spectators. No-one had thought to take a raincoat or umbrella. They all rushed back to the coach, ladies to the rear, men to the front, and all proceeded to disrobe. The coach soon looked like a laundry, as dresses, shirts and trousers were neatly draped over the seats to dry. By the time we got back to Leicester, the sun was shining and the clothes, although still a bit damp, were at least wearable.

Another trip which ended in a soaking was to the Henley Regatta. I had a coach full of twenty- to thirty-year-olds, all dressed up for the day. They stowed a crate of champagne and a picnic in the boot. It was a beautiful day and the youngsters were out to enjoy themselves. They insisted that I joined them for a picnic, minus

Champagne for me, of course, and it was then that I noticed two of the men were getting quite drunk as they each tried to outdo each other in the drinking stakes. I went to Charlie, who was nominally in charge, and warned him that if the two lads got too drunk and rowdy, I might have to leave them behind for safety reasons. So Charlie went to talk to the tipsy two, but unfortunately, one of the drunks did not like being told to lay off the booze and he took a swing at Charlie – big mistake. Charlie ducked; the drunk chap lost his balance and tottered into the Thames with a huge splash, accompanied by a huge cheer from the crowd!

It is amazing how quickly a person can sober up when dipped in cold water. The others pulled him out of the river and he was immediately sick on the grass (better than in my coach). He was soaking wet, of course, so I was reluctant to let him on to the coach, but a solution came to me. I always kept a pair of overalls on the coach in case I had to do any maintenance, so I offered these to the lad and he was only too glad to get into something dry. His clothes were draped over the boot lid and dried out in the sunshine.

Methinks another lesson was learned that day.

I did many runs to the East Coast resorts, and one particular trip to Mablethorpe comes to mind. Fred and I took a couple of coach-loads of people, some of whom were mums and dads who were visiting their offspring in the children's holiday home there. The holiday home was a charity which gave children in needy homes their only chance for a short holiday by the sea. We arrived at about 11.30am and didn't have to leave until 5.30pm, so we had quite a few hours to fill.

Now, Fred was a keen photographer and wanted to take some interesting views of the area, so we wandered along the seafront until we came to the amusement park. It was early in the season, May, and many of the stall holders were just preparing their stalls. Fred suddenly had a good idea, or so we thought at the time. We asked the man in charge of the big wheel if we could be sent up to the top to get some aerial shots. The man readily agreed, and as there were no other passengers, we climbed into a gondola and up we went. Fred took his snaps, and we called down to the man to let us down. The wheel started to move, and round we went, round and round and round. It was as we were going up for the fourth time that we realised the whole place was deserted – everyone had gone for lunch. The first twenty turns were quite pleasant, with the blue sky, light sea breeze and the quiet, but the next twenty was when we began to feel worried. It was not until the next twenty rotations that panic began to niggle at our insides, or was that hunger? We lost count after that, but it must have been approaching a hundred turns when the man returned to let us off.

"Did you enjoy your ride? I just went for a quick cuppa," he quipped, with a grin. I have never been on a big wheel since.

I have always been inquisitive, wanting to know what is on the other side of the hill, so on a day trip to Bala Lake in Wales, I had a chance to explore. It was a lovely day, and, having had a good look at a map beforehand, I had seen that there was a road right round the lake, albeit unclassified on the east side, so I told my passengers that they were in for a scenic treat, as I was taking them right round the lake. The first part of the trip was very pleasant, with quite a reasonable road and beautiful scenery, but on the other side, things began to get a bit tight. The road became narrow, and before long, the hedges were brushing the sides of the coach. The road in front looked like a small green tunnel. On the next bend we met a rather surprised-looking car driver, who very kindly reversed about a quarter of a mile so that we could pass. Needless to say, the coach was covered with scratches. I had to work a long time that night in the depot, polishing out the scratches with Brasso (metal polish). You could do that on the old hand brush-painted vehicles, but don't try it on your new car!

Nowadays, bus cleaning involves high-pressure spray guns and steam cleaning. The first time I took a bus to be steam cleaned, there appeared to be a space man standing in the pit, covered from head to toe in waterproof coveralls, goggles, gloves and a mask. It was the steam cleaner, and when he had finished, the underside of the bus was spotless, but he was… well, you can imagine the dirt!

Another occasion comes to mind when my coach needed a good clean. I had to travel up to Aberdeen to collect a coach and drive it back to Leicester. A new motorway had just opened, so it was quicker for me to travel via Carlisle, fill up with fuel there, drive over Shap Fells and pick up the road to the south. On the approach to Shap Fells from the North it was raining and I noticed that the white lines on the road were pink. I thought that perhaps my eyesight was playing tricks on me because I was tired, so I pulled into a layby for a break. After a micro nap, I set off again – the white lines were definitely pink! Glancing to my right, in a field, were *pink sheep*! A bit further up the road I discovered the reason. I wasn't going mad after all. Two lorries had collided, one of which had been carrying powdered pink dye. It had shed its load, and the weather conditions of strong wind and rain had scattered the dye far and wide. There were pink police cars and pink firemen trying to wash the pink dye from the road. I continued my journey with a pink windscreen and was the butt of many jokes when I turned up at the depot with a decidedly pink coach. Hooray for the cleaners.

That was Shap Fells in summer, but winter up there could be treacherous. Ask any long-distance driver. One winter, a mate of mine had to leave his vehicle as night approached because the road was blocked. All the regular lorry drivers had long since abandoned their trucks and made their way to the nearest village, Shap, to get accommodation. They knew from experience that they had to get in early to find a bed for the night. My mate had left it a bit late, and as he went from house to house he feared he would have nowhere to stay. However, he was advised by one householder to go down to Mrs Brown's house, as she took in the Eskimos and should have room. He was intrigued; surely the weather wasn't that bad? When he arrived at Mrs Brown's, he discovered that she really did cater for Eskimos – the drivers of the Eskimo Frozen food chain. Enough of the cold, let's have summer.

I remember taking a thirty-seat long-distance coach from Leicester to Great Yarmouth. It was a six-cylinder, petrol-driven job; owing to the design, the driver sat almost on top of the fuel tank, with the engine at the side of one's left leg. This got hotter and hotter as the journey progressed. I climbed up the iron ladder at the rear of the bus to stow some of the passengers' luggage on the roof, because there was no boot or luggage compartment. A few items would not fit, so I found room for them inside the coach, in a specially designed box situated just behind the engine housing. At the end of the journey, I noticed a lot of liquid all over the floor by the luggage box. Someone had packed 2lb of butter in their suitcase, and it had melted, soaking all of their clothes.

A similar occurrence happened many years later. Whilst on a visit to my daughter in Suffolk, we decided to go to an air show at an American base at Mildenhall. The day before, 1st June, we had had a freak snowstorm, but the day of our trip dawned warm and sunny, with a beautiful blue sky. We had arranged to meet friends, Mary and Donald, with their children. By the time we arrived at the venue, the temperature was climbing up towards twenty-seven degrees. We spent some time looking at displays, then returned to our cars for a picnic, with the temperature now nudging twenty-nine degrees. Mary opened the boot of their car – it was running with melted butter, and the cheese was so sweaty she could barely cut it with a knife, but she managed to salvage something. After lunch we needed to buy more drink because of the heat – the Yanks had it covered. They had a huge chill cabinet filled with light beer and cola, which they were selling as fast as possible, handing out cans with one hand and taking money with the other (they charged fifty cents or fifty pence). I have never seen drink move so fast, but with great military proficiency, as soon as supplies began to get low, a van pulled up with fresh supplies. By now the temperature had topped thirty-two degrees and the heat by the runway was almost unbearable, so we made our way to the aircraft parked for display and found some shade standing under their wings. This was the start of the long hot summer of 1976.

I thought I had reached the peak of my job as a coach driver, when the firm increased their fleet with some super new coaches for use on extended tours, and once again I was chosen to join the select few. We were known as the three Cs – Coach Cruise Couriers. We had navy-blue suits tailor made and were issued with three white shirts and a company tie. I remember my first cruise, which was for one week. Starting in Leicester, touring North Wales, the Lake District and the Yorkshire Dales, staying in the best hotels, for a grand total of £18 all in.

It was a new beginning for me.

Coronation

I cannot pass through the 1950s without mentioning the coronation. In 1953, the whole nation was in the grip of coronation fever. We had come through the war and austerity was coming to a close. A beautiful young woman was about to be crowned queen, heralding the start of a new Elizabethan age, a new beginning, full of promise for a brighter future.

I may have mentioned before about our acquisition of a television set just before the late King's funeral, when half the street came to watch the event. Well, the same happened again. We invited neighbours in to watch the coverage, which went from 11.00am for several hours (at least five hours, if I remember correctly). People brought sandwiches with them and Alice provided cups of tea and glasses of orange squash. We had arranged a street a party for later in the day, but unfortunately, it was a wet day. However, Alice had had the presence of mind to pre-book the local church hall, just in case, so we had a party after all.

Someone in the street had suggested, a few months before, that we should have a street outing to Skegness to celebrate this important event. We all agreed, and guess who was chosen to be the coach driver? The Coronation was on a Tuesday, so it was decided to make the outing on the following Saturday, when most people were not at work.

The day for the trip arrived, rather grey but dry. Everyone stowed their picnics and eagerly climbed aboard. We set off with a loud cheer, followed by excited chattering. Now, remember, only a short time before, the East Coast had suffered terrible flooding and was still trying to get back to normal, but this didn't dampen the enthusiasm of the crowd, who were determined to have a good time, come what may.

We duly arrived without mishap and immediately families headed for the beach. The tide was *out*! If you know Skeggy, then you will be familiar with the fact that the tide goes out for miles! I have been to Skegness many times but have only been twice when the tide was right in. On this occasion, the children were happy enough building sandcastles, playing cricket or running races on the wet sand. There were a few fairground rides open for the more adventurous of us. The day went very well and a good time was had by all.

Also during the Coronation period, schoolchildren were given a commemorative mug and a Bible. I remember the girls coming home from school, telling us how they had been practising singing, "God Save the Queen". It seemed strange not to sing King instead of Queen, but we soon got used to it. Pageants were organised and concerts performed. Everyone decorated their houses or places of work – the country was awash with red, white and blue. We even grew red, white and blue flowers in our gardens, and, of course, we dressed in red, white and blue for the parties and trips.

It was a good time to be alive, and it really was a new beginning.

A brief footnote to the Coronation. Many years later, we were invited to visit one of the grooms who lived at the Royal Mews, Buckingham Palace. During the afternoon, he took us on a private tour of the mews to see all of the carriages, including the Golden Coach. We had a good look round, and then, the highlight of the trip, whilst the groom kept cavy by the door, I helped Alice up into the Coronation Coach and climbed up to sit beside her. After a couple of photos and a few royal waves, we climbed down again, feeling like naughty children but very happy – what an experience. It is a magnificent piece of craftsmanship, beautifully carved, gilded and painted. Inside there was a small cradle to hold the orb after the Coronation, because such a heavy object would have been too heavy for Her Majesty to hold all the way back to the Palace. The Queen's seat seemed to be a little further forward than Prince Phillip's and was quite comfortable, but evidently travel in the coach was rather rock and roll.

I wonder how many other members of the public have sat in the Coronation Coach, and have photos to prove it, and have not ended up in the Tower of London.

With the advent of private hire of coaches, I had quite a few unusual trips. One such was a Sikh wedding.

During the 1950s, we saw a number of Sikhs employed by the company. I often had a Sikh conductor working with me, whose name was Baljinder Singh, and he spoke quite good English. He was a very pleasant chap, very polite and with a good sense of humour, so we got on very well. I was interested in his religion and culture, and I did my best to advise him on things he wanted to know about Western culture. He had been born in the Punjab but had spent most of his early life in Kenya. Some of the other staff were racist and didn't want to work with these "foreigners", but I think this was just ignorance and fear of the unknown. I was brought up to treat people as I would wish to be treated, so I was delighted to be asked to drive a bus full of Sikhs to a wedding in Birmingham.

Baljinder asked for me specially, because, and I quote, "You are such a decent fellow." I turned up at the allotted place and marvelled at the beautiful outfits the people were wearing. The guests filled the boot and racks with wedding gifts, and we set off for Birmingham. When we arrived, I was amazed to be treated as a guest of honour. I felt like a king, especially when they produced a beautifully made head covering for me. Also, I had my first taste of Indian food – it was fantastic!

I learned since that Sikhs have a great tradition of hospitality, and if you go to a gurdwara (Sikh temple) you will always be offered food. I believe it is the same in a Hindu temple (mandir). There is certainly a lot we could learn from other religions and cultures. I wonder why we don't see the same good aspects of other religions, rather than the differences.

The world would be a dull place if we were all the same.

Chapter Seven
Hub Caps and High Water

I had a call to say that one of our buses was stuck in floodwater midway between two villages – all hands to the rescue. We loaded up a spare bus with shovels, tow chains, waders, exhaust extension, blankets and flasks of hot tea. We eventually arrived at a desolate scene – a lake of floodwater with sheets of ice floating in it, and there, in the middle, a double-decker bus. How on earth had he got that far?

We donned our waders and made our way gingerly to the rear of the bus to fit the exhaust extension and the tow chains. One of the rescue party volunteered to go round to the marooned driver to give him instructions. As he came level with the driver's window, he suddenly disappeared beneath the water; he had forgotten about the roadside ditch. We hurried as fast as the water would allow and pulled him out, spluttering and shaking, and escorted him to terra firma, where we laid him on the ground and lifted him up by his feet to drain the water from his waders. Then we wrapped him in blankets and plied him with hot tea. After we had rescued the stricken bus, we quickly took the shivering chap back to the depot, but no sooner had we returned than we were sent out on another mercy mission. This time, the driver of the marooned bus was a real hero. He had carried his passengers on his back, to dry land, before calling for help.

One morning it was my turn to be a flood victim. The road I was using was prone to flooding, and, with care, usually posed no problems, except on this occasion. The road was flooded with about two feet of water, for about four hundred yards, but what I hadn't realised was that during the night there had been a particularly hard frost. The water level had dropped, leaving a very, very thick sheet of suspended ice, and as soon as my front wheels were over the ice, there was a tremendous crack and my bus collapsed through it onto the road below with a huge jolt. I thought my axle had bust, but luck was with me. Thank goodness for sturdy buses.

I had a very brave mate who had got himself stuck in a flood, with the water still rising and gushing into the bus, a single-decker. As the water level rose, the passengers climbed on to the back of the seats and the driver stripped off his uniform and boots, plunged into the icy water and swam to get help. What a hero!

These local floods were just a mild annoyance compared to the East Coast floods of 1952. I was on standby in the garage when the call came through from the local police asking for a coach and driver to take a group of police officers to Sutton-on-Sea to help with rescue and policing duties following the catastrophic flooding. I had this job every five days during the emergency, sometimes collecting officers from Coventry, Birmingham and Leicester. These trips also involved driving to Cadbury's at Bourneville to pick up a cargo of chocolate, which was to help sustain the helpers in this difficult time.

On my first trip, I drove as close to the coast as possible, then local farmers ferried us, using tractors and trailers, to where we were needed most urgently.

Gradually the water subsided, and we could get coaches to the town as long as we kept between the iron posts which had been hammered into the ground to mark the edge of the road, which was still covered with water. To deviate from the route would have been disastrous. Straw and debris hung in the branches of trees many feet from the ground. I shall never forget the sight of so many houses full of wet sand to the height of about four feet – how could they clear that? Imagine a lorry load of wet sand being tipped into your living room, all over your furniture and treasured possessions – what a nightmare! Before the floods there had been huge sand dunes at Sutton, but now they were in people's houses. The police HQ was in a hotel, next door to which was a rest home. To get to the door, one had to tread carefully down a sandy slope, but after the clearing operation, one had to go along a path and up a flight of six steps to get to the door after the floods. A fine new promenade was later built at Sutton, but it took many years for that stretch of coast to recover.

On a much smaller scale, an incident, concerning rescue from water, happened one Sunday afternoon, and it had a profound influence on me. When I wasn't working, my wife and I used to love taking our girls to Abbey Park, dressed in our Sunday best. We would take a picnic, with spare bread to feed the ducks, and sometimes we would spend half an hour on the boating lake, or wander around the ruins of Leicester Abbey, or go and look at the birds in the aviary. One day, we finished our picnic and were walking by the lake when we saw a young lad fall into the water on the other shore. Now, the lake was not deep, but the boy was panicking, and by the way he was thrashing about, it was obvious he could not swim.

I started running round the lake to rescue him, as no-one seemed to be aware of the accident. As I neared the place where the boy was struggling, someone else beat me to it, and he jumped in and dragged the boy out, alive and creating "blue murder" – thank goodness, he was very much alive, although very shaken and stirred! His parents appeared on the scene, very upset, and it was hugs all round. Alice admitted later that she was very concerned about me spoiling my only suit but at the same time was pleased to have such a hero as a husband. A tragedy was avoided, but it had a deep impact on me, so I decided there and then that our girls would learn to swim properly. I enrolled them in Belgrave Swimming Club.

Alice found it difficult taking the girls because she was absolutely terrified of water following an incident when she was young, and she didn't like watching them diving into deep water, in case they didn't surface again. Luckily they were old enough to go by themselves.

When she was a girl, Alice had been walking home from school with her sisters Rose and Lily, the twins. It was a freezing, cold day and the Lincolnshire dykes (ditches) had a thick layer of ice on them. Forgetting all about her parents' repeated warnings concerning the dangers of going through the ice, Alice decided that she would have a go at sliding on the ice; after all, it was very thick. So she stepped carefully and was feeling triumphant, because for a while, the ice held her weight, then *crack*! The ice gave way, and Alice went through into the icy water below and disappeared from sight. The twins began to scream, but fortune was on their side, in the shape of their neighbour's big, strapping son who was cycling home from work.

He immediately saw what had happened, threw his bike on to the frozen grass, lay down on the ground next to the dyke and put his long arm into the icy water; by some miracle, he managed to grab hold of Alice's hair and gave it a pull. As soon as he had her head above water, he was able to grab her coat and heave her out of the dyke, coughing and spluttering but alive. This near-drowning experience had put her off deep water for the rest of her life.

When I was young, it was not common for people to learn to swim, which seems strange for people living on an island. My brother, Alfred, came to the rescue, as usual. He had learned to swim in the Scouts, mainly using the river. So he showed me the basics. I managed a rough breaststroke, which served me well. I was rather ungainly, but at least I could stay afloat and move through the water. I always kept my glasses on so that I could see where I was going, but had to try and keep my face dry, which somewhat limited the strokes I could do.

Other disasters come to mind, but not involving water. I was on a normal service run one day, being held up in a small traffic jam, when I noticed that the car in front of me was emitting smoke. The driver jumped out, and as he did so, the whole vehicle burst into flames, and I watched in amazement as the body of a little three-wheeled car turned to ash, in minutes, leaving just a blackened chassis on the road. It was one of those vehicles with a fibre-glass body. It didn't rust, but my, how it burned! My conductor had the presence of mind to jump off the bus and wave the traffic back so that I could reverse away from the fire. By the time a local shopkeeper came running with a fire extinguisher, it was all over.

Some months later, I was on the same route, when there was another hold-up. A learner driver, a young lady, had stalled her car in the middle of a busy junction. Other drivers became impatient, honking their horns. Now, immediately behind the learner was a police car and then me in my bus. The police could see that the poor young lady was getting very upset, so one of the officers used the loud hailer to call on drivers to be patient, "Because we were learners once," he said. Everything went quiet, until the girl put her car into reverse by mistake and went slamming into the police car. The officer, forgetting that the loud hailer was still switched on, came over loud and clear, saying, "What the b***** h*** is she doing now!" There were red faces that day, and for once it wasn't mine.

Chapter Eight
Accidents Will Happen

In all my years on the buses, I had very little time off through ill health, but when I did, it was something major.

One cold winter morning, when I was on early shift, I was walking from home to the main road so that I could catch the early bus. I heard it coming in the distance, there being no other traffic around at the time, so it was quiet. Not wanting to miss it, otherwise I would be fined for being late, I started to run. Suddenly, I tripped on an uneven paving slab and down I went. Unable to save myself, with hands deep in my great coat pockets, I crashed face first into a lamp post. I remember coming round, lying on the pavement, with a man bending over me saying the ridiculous words, "Are you alright, mate?"

As I sat up, covered in blood, he hurried off. I picked up my broken specs, pulled my handkerchief from my pocket to stench the flow of blood from my nose and mouth, then staggered home, with blood dripping all over my gloves and down the front of my coat. I let myself into my house and sat down in the kitchen, feeling rather faint and thinking, *It's a good job the floor tiles are red, they won't show the bloodstains.*

"Is that you, Percy?" called my wife.

"I've had a little accident," I mumbled. Alice came downstairs, took one look at me and fainted into the living room – she never could stand the sight of blood.

My eldest daughter then appeared on the scene and said, "What happened to you?"

I replied rather weakly, "I fell over."

She fetched the first aid kit and, with a little help from my wife, who had now recovered a little, cleaned me up a bit. It was obvious that I needed hospital care, so my wife popped round to a neighbour to see if he would be willing to drive me to hospital in my car. He agreed and off we went – me in the passenger seat, which I had never travelled in before, and Alice in the back, secretly wishing she wouldn't faint in the hospital. Ann stayed behind to look after her little sister when she woke up. Luckily it was Saturday, so there was no school. The girls cleaned up the kitchen so that there was no trace of blood to be seen. Well done, Ann and Susan!

In hospital, the X-ray showed that I had broken and split my nose, which needed stitching. My glasses had cut my face, which needed stitching, and my dentures had cut the inside of my mouth, which needed stitching – what a mess. The stitches in my mouth were extremely painful, but the thought that it could have been worse gave me strength to carry on. How could it have been worse, I hear you ask? The glass from my specs may have cut my face but missed my eyes by a fraction of an inch – I could have been blinded. Also, they were not my own teeth that had got smashed. I find it often pays to look on the bright side of life. I looked like I had done a few rounds with Henry Cooper, so I was kept in overnight for observation. The next morning, having shown no signs of concussion, I was allowed home, where I had to have a diet of mush because with the stitches, I couldn't bite or chew anything for a couple of weeks. I found that one of my favourite foods was very soothing – *jelly*, mmm!

Talking of accidents takes me back to my youth. I shall tell you how eating gooseberries broke my arm.

Some friends and I were playing out, when we decided to scrump a few gooseberries, from an allotment, which we shoved into our pockets until we found a good spot to sit and eat them.

We climbed up on to a high wall, and I popped a gooseberry into my mouth. Now, I had never eaten a raw gooseberry before, only ones cooked with sugar and usually in the form of crumble, with sweet custard. Well, the gooseberry in my mouth was so sour that I did a sharp intake of breath, overbalanced and fell backwards off the wall, breaking my arm. I have never touched a gooseberry since.

The second time I broke my arm was years later, when I was trying to start a car. In those days, it was commonplace to use a handle to manually crank start a cold engine. Well, I inserted the handle into the correct position and gave it a heave, but unfortunately, it kicked back and caught me smartly on the arm, which went with a loud crack. After three weeks in plaster, I had to have it reset, and that hurt more than the break. That was another lesson learned.

I do sound rather accident-prone, but none of these incidents were as bad as the day I nearly killed my brother and myself. I was sixteen, and my brother Alf was twenty-one. We decided to borrow our other brother's motorbike. Jim was home from college, and he gave us permission, as long as we were careful and gave it a clean before returning it. Now, expecting a sixteen-year-old lad to be careful is a bit of wishful thinking. I was driving and Alfred was riding pillion. In those days, safety equipment was unheard of, so off we went. We went speeding along the roads, with the bike going like a dream, when I took a corner too wide and too fast, and collided with the front end of a bus! Alfred shot off the pillion seat, over my head, and crashed into the bus, then rebounded onto the road. I remember regaining consciousness, with a woman cutting my trousers off my legs as I lay in the road.

Most of my injuries were deep cuts and gravel scrapes, but poor Alfred was in a bad way. We were both taken to hospital, where I soon recovered, but my brother had a fight to get back to health. Luckily, he made a full recovery, apart from some bad scars. The bike was a complete write-off and the front axle of the bus was broken, so you can imagine the impact. We were certainly very

Percy's Bus

lucky to be alive. That was the first and last road accident that was my fault in over sixty years.

Another time I ended up in hospital was due to crazy paving. I was creating a crazy pavement in the garden at home, which entailed breaking slabs with a big hammer and chisel. A splinter shot up from the slab and, by-passing my specs, landed in my eye. It was exceedingly painful, and I could not get it out, as it was firmly stuck to my eye, even after washing the eye with copious amounts of water. Once again, a neighbour came to the rescue, and with me holding a clean handkerchief over my eye, I was driven to the emergency unit at the hospital. The doctor soon removed the offending piece of concrete, put stinging drops in the eye and swathed a dressing round my head to keep the patch in place. So I had a few more days off work but, once again, learned a new lesson.

At least I fared better than my wife's grandfather. As an agricultural worker, he was skilled in various rural crafts, including hedge laying. He was chopping away one day, when a branch of the hawthorn that he was laying swung back and hit him in the eye, damaging it so severely that he had to have his eye removed because it was beyond repair. After that, he had a glass eye, and if you sat on his left side, he often did not see what you were doing. We once sat down for dinner and watched in horror as he devoured a caterpillar which was on the lettuce on his blind side. No-one dared say a word!

I had another lesson to learn at work. I was in the club room at work, where the staff could meet for a cuppa or a game of cards or darts (no gambling allowed), and I was sitting chatting to a mate who had his dog with him. His dog, an Alsatian, was usually quite docile, and I used to make a fuss of him, so he knew me quite well. Unfortunately, on this occasion, I said, "Where's the cats, boy?", not knowing that the dog always reacted badly to the word cats. The dog snarled and sank his teeth into the back of my hand, drawing a flow of blood. My mate was upset, but it wasn't his fault; I should have had more sense – another lesson learned. Once again it was off to the hospital, this time on a bus, with my hand dressed by the first aid person at work. The staff at the hospital checked out the injuries and said I was lucky that no tendons were damaged, so they patched me up and sent me home. I had to take a couple of weeks off work until the hand had healed.

Chapter Nine
Percy in Newark

Me in sailor suit with Mother and brothers James and Alfred, 1915

When I was a boy in Newark, my friends and I used to hang around the breweries watching the activities. We particularly liked to see the huge dray horses, in all their finery, clattering to and from the yard. Through the cellar windows we could see the men raking the hops in the water. They waded barefoot, with trousers rolled up to their knees, and combed through the hops with huge wooden rakes. Their boots were placed on the cellar windowsills (at street level), for safekeeping, or so they thought, but we crept up and poked the boots with a long stick until they fell into the mixture below. I can honestly say that I have never enjoyed a pint of best bitter, thinking of corns, calluses and stinking boots!

When we tired of the brewery, we roamed around the town, kicking a tin can, or perhaps throwing stones into the river, seeing who could make the biggest splash. Depending on the group mood, we might make model boats out of bits and pieces we found, and watch until they either sank or disappeared downstream. Occasionally, we'd chase each other with dog excrement on a stick (aren't small boys delightful?). More about dog excrement later.

Sometimes we went to where the houses had opposing "front" doors down a passageway. We tied the two front doors together very stealthily with a bit of old rope, then knocked and ran. We hid not too far away so that we could hear the struggle as neighbours tried to open their doors, whilst gagging our giggles.

Other times, when it was dark, and the gas streetlamps had been lit, we would fasten a small weight to a length of black thread, filched from mother's sewing basket, and pin this to the sash window of some unsuspecting neighbour. We hid in their entry (side passage), gave a few tugs on the thread and the little weight tapped the window. Time and again the people pulled back their curtain to see who was there but would see just an empty street. We thought this was hilarious. We were only caught once, and had our ears soundly boxed for our trouble. But for all our mischief, we never damaged property or hurt anyone, except their pride.

One favourite trick, which was very unpleasant for the recipient, was carried out mainly in the winter, when the evenings were dark. We spread dog excrement on to the latch of someone's back gate, then carefully placed a drawing pin, point side up, on the top. The man of the house would come home from work, go to open the gate with his thumb on the latch, get a severe prick of the thumb, swear, then automatically put his thumb in his mouth for relief. From our concealed hiding place we found this extremely funny. Little boys, eh?

From the vile taste to the delicious.

I had a great liking for pickled walnuts. My mother used to make a lot of preserves in the autumn, such as jam, pickled red cabbage, pickled onions and pickled walnuts. They were placed very high up on the top shelf of the pantry, ready for Christmas. However, when no-one was around, I would creep into the pantry, climb precariously up to the top shelf and pop a pickled walnut into my mouth.

Somehow I never got caught but can still remember the look of surprise on my mother's face when she found that the jar of walnuts was empty, apart from the vinegar. She had no idea that I had scaled the heights of the pantry, and I wasn't going to tell, so we had to make do with pickled onions that year.

As a young lad, my brothers and I, with numerous friends, ran fairly wild. We had great pleasure in building bonfires on derelict land on the edge of town and trying to cook potatoes in a rusty old tin. Sometimes, we went down to the railway and put a penny or halfpenny on the line so that we could see the train squash it out of shape. What a waste of a penny – but it amused us.

Other times we went fishing for "tiddlers" in the river with a bent pin on the end of a piece of string, which was attached to a stick. (We always seemed to be in possession of a piece of string and a stick.) We never caught anything, except the odd piece of water weed. One day, we saw a dead fish floating by and managed to hook it out of the water, then spent the next half hour chasing each other around with the rotting fish on a stick, until its head fell off.

When we moved to Lincoln, one of our favourite occupations was scrumping apples (scrumping – taking fruit without the owner's permission), which were invariably sour to eat, but we didn't mind, because it was part of the adventure. Sometimes, we filled our pockets with the apples, went to the prison and threw them over the prison wall, which was not very high, or climbed a nearby tree and shouted and waved to the prisoners, who were highly amused by the antics of these young lads. We always kept a lookout for warders, because I am sure we would have had our ears boxed if we had been caught.

When one of the group managed to get hold of a ball, we'd go to the common for a game of football, taking great care not to step or fall on one of numerous cow pats. However, part of the game was trying to push or pull a mate into one. No wonder we called the common the cow paddle.

When we first moved to Lincoln from Newark, we lived in a terraced house built on the side of a steep hill. One day, some relatives were visiting, with an old aunt in a bath chair – you may know the sort, if you are an older reader, the type made out of wickerwork, with two wheels at the back and one wheel at the front attached to a tiller for steering. This conveyance was parked carefully at the front of the house, because it was too awkward to manoeuvre it inside or down the side entry. My brothers and I decided to keep out of the way of the adults until teatime, when we would be summoned indoors, and thought it might be fun to give each other a push round in the bath chair. It was very hard work, so after a few goes, we decided to run it down the hill for a bit of speed – just like a toboggan. We hadn't lived on a hill before so didn't think things through. It was great fun as we hurtled down the hill (which was very steep) faster and faster, but there was one thing we had all forgotten – no brakes!

Actually, there was a rudimentary parking brake which was no match for something moving at speed. We hung on for dear life, with the bath chair wobbling crazily from side to side, as we approached the junction at the bottom of the hill. We shot off the kerb and somersaulted onto the road in a heap of arms and legs.

Luckily there was no traffic in those days, so we just sported cuts, grazes and bruises. We were badly shaken and bloody, but miraculously, in one piece, which was more than could be said for the chair. The front wheel was hideously bent – what could we do? We were surely in for a good thrashing! Alf to the rescue. He suggested taking the chair along the road to the blacksmith, who just happened to be the father of a friend of his. We dragged the chair along to his forge, and we must have looked a pathetic sight, because he picked up his tools, with a big grin on his face, and proceeded to fix the wheel. He did a first-class repair job and refused any payment. He also let us into his kitchen so that we could clean ourselves up a bit.

Every time he saw us after that, he gave us a big grin and winked his eye. We heaved the chair back up the hill, parked it very carefully and waited to be summoned for tea. We had to wash again before we presented ourselves before the family, but that was a small price to pay for our close call. No-one commented on the cuts and bruises, because they were normal occurrences for three lively lads, and the family never did find out what had happened.

School was not really my scene, except for art and story writing (I've always had a vivid imagination). So one morning, I decided to bunk off. I was very young, so it was the responsibility of my two older brothers, Alfred and Jim, to escort me to my primary school on the way to their school. On this particular morning I ran away from them and hid for a while until they had passed by. When the coast was clear, I doubled back home. Alfred and Jim thought I'd run on ahead to school so did not bother to check – pesky kid brother! I let myself into the house very quietly (people tended to leave doors unlocked in those days). I collected my favourite toy train from the cupboard and hid under the table, which was draped with a long cloth – tabletop to floor. I was there for quite a while making up stories about my train and was so engrossed in my fantasy train world that I forgot where I was and was discovered by my aunt, who lived with us, when she heard a "chuff chuff chuffing" coming from under the table. The game was up!

I was given a smack and sent to my room to await my father's punishment when he came home. It was a very long wait. Luckily for me, my father was a gentleman in every meaning of the word, so he gave me a good talking-to on how I had let everyone down, especially myself. He hoped I could make amends to everyone I had upset. His solution was that I should write a letter of apology to my teacher, the headteacher, my mother, my aunt and my father.

Five letters! It took me ages but taught me a valuable lesson – every action has a reaction. I never bunked off again. As for Alf and Jim, they had a roasting from father about their responsibilities. Ah, happy days.

Chapter Ten
Busman's Holiday

Father paddling in suit and hat

When I was a boy, my family used to holiday in resorts such as Scarborough. Mother and Father, my mother's sister, Eva, my two brothers and me. We all dressed up in our best clothes – my father in his three-piece suit with a trilby hat, and my mother in a summer dress, with straw hat. The only concession to the seaside was a pair of beach shoes – i.e. canvas deck shoes. Even us lads had to wear fairly formal clothes. I was allowed short knee-length trousers, whilst my older brothers were allowed light-coloured flannels (trousers) and blazers, and they were not required to wear a hat. We seemed to spend a lot of time parading up and down the promenade, and sometimes the adults hired a deck chair on the beach or by the bandstand. I have a vivid memory of my father removing his shoes and socks, rolling up his trousers as far as his knees and paddling in the water, but still wearing his full suit and hat. I too was allowed to paddle knee-deep. The best holidays were where there were rock pools on the beach, because that would keep me occupied for a few hours. I also enjoyed going to the theatre at the end of the pier or to the Winter Gardens. I suppose we were lucky to be able to take a break, and it wasn't too bad really, as my older brothers were given the task of keeping me entertained.

Living in Lincolnshire, we were able to take day trips by train, to the coast, to Mablethorpe or Skegness. I remember in later years a trip to Skegness, with friends. We went on the boating lake, but after about ten minutes, Alice's friend, Gladys, became really seasick, and we had to let her off the boat. How can anyone be seasick in two feet of water?

That reminds me of a trip to the Isle of Man. Not long after we were married, Alice and I saved up to go to the Isle of Man with Alice's sister Flo and her husband Horace. The sea was not rough – just a gentle swell – so although Alice and Flo were a little queasy, they were not too bad; Horace and I seemed OK. All was well until we stepped ashore. Horace, after a few minutes on terra firma, was violently sick. It appeared that he was land-sick. He never did live that down.

The next time we went to the Isle of Man was in 1946, just after the war. The girls were young, and it was a big adventure for them, going on the ferry. The sea was very rough, so Alice and Ann stayed in the cabin feeling grotty and trying not to be sick, but I stayed on deck, because I like nothing better than a rough sea. Susan, who was four years old, was on her feet for most of the journey, going between me on deck or in the bar and the others below. She seemed to have inherited my love of stormy waters and obviously had good sea legs, because she never tripped once, in spite of the heaving deck. Other passengers were highly amused to see this little dot making her way around the ferry in quite a fearless fashion. We had a good holiday even though the weather was rather dull and a little wet for the week we were there. We went on the horse-drawn tram which the girls loved; we built sandcastles, looked in rock pools and waved to the fairies from the bridge. What more could you want?

Our next holiday was at Huttoft, on the East Coast. We hired a static caravan and went with our next-door neighbours, who had a teenage boy and a daughter the same age as Susan. This time we had good weather.

Following that, we went to Gorleston on the Norfolk coast for several years, with some very good friends of ours. They had two daughters the same ages as our two, so we had some great holidays. The weather was usually kind to us in early June, and we spent many happy hours on the beach and in the sea. We all got on well and had similar interests. When we went to Gorleston, we stayed in digs with Mr and Mrs Bush, who were a really delightful couple, and our friends stayed across the road. Mrs Bush was an excellent cook, and we looked forward to the meals she prepared with the food we bought. At the time, some food was still on ration, so we used to shop and she used to cook.

The girls were amused by the quaint outside toilet, which consisted of a smooth oak plank across the hole, with a neatly fitting lid, which had a handle on it so that it could be removed when required. The toilet had a flushing device, but it just looked like something out of the ark. Susan was also fascinated by the coloured glass panels in the door which opened into our sitting room (the front parlour of the house) and would spend ages looking through the different-coloured panes.

Mr Bush worked on the dredger in Yarmouth harbour and was also the coxswain of the lifeboat, so whenever we were near and he was on duty, we used to go into the station and have a look round. Wherever we were, when we heard the maroon go off, we knew Mr Bush would be on his way to man the lifeboat. The girls took a shine to Mr Bush; he was like another grandpa to them and he would amuse Susan by singing "Susie Green". Also, because he was well known in Gorleston, we were also invited to visit the coastguard station, where they would explain the weather cones, show us the charts or allow us to look through the telescope, which was so powerful that you could see every detail inside the caravans across the river, as well as ships on the horizon.

Whilst at Gorleston, we spent a great deal of time on the beach, because we usually had good weather in early June. Sometimes we would venture into the outdoor pool and always attended the water spectacular they held there in the season, with synchronised swimming, water ballet and slapstick clowns somersaulting off the high boards into the water below.

The girls liked to buy pink and white ice creams from the Italian ice-cream parlour, using some of their pocket money. Susan was desperate to buy a knickerbocker glory, but they cost half a crown, which was a whole week's budget, so for the whole holiday, apart from the pink and white ice cream, she saved her money, instead of spending on souvenirs or sweets. On the last day of the holiday, we took her into the shop and told the proprietor how she had saved up her money, and he was so impressed, he gave her the treat for nothing! Her dream came true – she ate the lot!

If the weather was not so good, as sometimes happened at high tide, we would take a boat trip to the Broads. I remember one trip as far as Beccles, where we stopped for afternoon tea in a barn. Scones and jam were part of the package, but no-one seemed to know what sort of jam it was, except that it was brown. An old pianola was cranked up for our entertainment, but unfortunately, it only had one roll of music – "Lambeth Walk". It played over and over again, and each time it reached the end of the roll, the whole piano would lurch with a loud bang and then begin again. It certainly entertained us, and we left the barn "doing the Lambeth Walk – bang!"

Another trip we made sometimes, was in the little rowing boat around the harbour wall from Gorleston Beach to Yarmouth harbour. The old man who rowed us was a retired fisherman, lean and weather-beaten. It was a hard pull round the end of the breakwater, and the girls were fascinated and perhaps a little frightened by the whirlpools where the river ran into the sea, but it was part of the adventure.

I just mentioned the sea wall. Well, there was a wooden breakwater built next to the wall, and when the sea breeze was a bit stiff, we would climb down into the wooden structure which was known as the Cosies, and enjoy our picnic, nice and cosy. One day when we were in the Cosies, there was a young couple a few feet away from us, and they started to quarrel. The row grew and grew, until the young man lost his temper, grabbed the girl's bag, tossed it into the sea and stormed off, leaving his young lady in tears. Dennis and I to the rescue. We grabbed our fishing lines and between us managed to hook the bag before it sank. We duly handed the bag to the girl. It was the only thing we ever caught.

The girls had a game where they jumped off the sea wall on to the beach below and would try to see who could go the furthest. The wall at Gorleston was about three feet high so posed no problem, especially with the soft landing. One day, we walked along the cliff top to Lowestoft, which had an identical sea wall, except that it was about twelve feet high. The girls ran ahead of us, and three of them stopped short, as they could see that there was a height difference, but poor Gwen leapt for all she was worth and disappeared from view. She scared the daylights out of a young couple who were sitting backed up to the wall, when she came flying over their heads. Luckily Gwen survived with just a sprained ankle, shock and bruised pride. What's that old adage? …Look before you leap!

After a few years going to Gorleston, we decided to have a change of venue, so Dennis and I organised a holiday to Hayling Island. We travelled by train, but when we reached our destination, we were somewhat shocked by the accommodation. We had seen pictures of the wooden chalets but had no idea that they were so small. Only one person at a time could go in through the door, because a bed was in the way. There was no room to swing a mouse round, let alone the proverbial cat, and we had to climb over each other to move round. To make matters worse, the food was not very good, not a patch on Mrs Bush's cooking. The only milk available was goat's milk, which was not popular with the girls; in fact, the whole complex reeked of the goats which the owner kept in the field next door. To make matters worse, the weather was not very kind to us.

When we had a good day, we headed for a beach, which we had great difficulty finding, because a lot of beaches were privately owned and most of the others were still guarded by barbed wire left over from the war. So, to make the best of a bad job, Dennis and I organised a trip to Portsmouth. We turned up at the station and took the train to Havant, where we had to change for Portsmouth. The stationmaster told us to take the next diesel train, but unfortunately, Dennis and I didn't listen properly, and we loaded our families on to the next train – a steam train – and ended up back on Hayling Island. We took the next train back to Havant, where the stationmaster greeted us with a grin, and queried, "What are you all doing here again?" So we caught the next diesel train to Portsmouth and made our way to see HMS *Victory*. It was quite a poignant moment when we stood by the spot where Nelson fell, because my family was connected to his through marriage.

After we had toured the *Victory*, we wandered round the docks looking at the numerous ships berthed there and decided to go and look at the submarines. Part of the area was fenced off, but there was a gap in the fence, so we all piled through and headed towards the sub pens. We hadn't gone very far when we were challenged by two armed navy guards, demanding to know what the h*** we were doing in this top-secret facility and how had we got there. After listening to our story, we were escorted back to whence we came and the fence was closed behind us. It was a good job we had our families with us, otherwise I think Den and I might have been arrested. Even though this holiday was not quite what we'd hoped for, we had many a laugh about it afterwards.

Years later, my wife was asked to help with the cooking at the girls' school camp, so that was to be our holiday. We went to Criccieth, near Porthmadog, in Wales, and it rained and poured and deluged! Never have I seen so much rain. My wife and the other cook spent the two weeks draped in towels to catch the drips from the tarpaulin covering the field kitchen. We had to dig trenches round the tents to keep out the water and lay sticks by the tent entrances to try and keep out the mud. We spent most of the time in wellies and shorts, because our legs were easier to dry than trousers. We still carried on with our usual activities, such as sports, treasure hunts, fancy-dress competitions, sea bathing and trips out.

Susan's group won a prize for their fancy dress. They gathered reeds from the sand dunes and made them into grass skirts, made garlands of flowers out of tissue paper, and went as South Sea Islanders, complete with a castaway – a young man they had found locally. It actually stopped raining just long enough to hold the parade.

Most days, a party of girls was escorted through the dunes to the sea to swim, as long as it was not too rough. The only problem with the sea bathing was getting the towels dry afterwards, but no-one complained. We even swam when it was raining. Well, we could hardly get any wetter than we were on land! Camp inspection every morning had to be adapted because the girls could not put their kit outside as per usual but stacked it neatly as possible inside the tents. Towards the end of the stay we managed a campfire evening, even though it was difficult to get a good fire going in the damp conditions, but where there's a will…

The local cinema manager heard about our plight and opened up his cinema especially for us one afternoon, for a free viewing, so we got a couple of hours sitting in the warm and dry, enjoying a film. Good Welsh hospitality!

Then came the day we had to travel home. We crowded on to the local station platform, waiting for our train, in which we had a reserved carriage, supposedly, but when the train arrived, it was completely packed and the stationmaster would not oust the people from our reserved carriage but told us to wait for the next train, which, he claimed, had plenty of spaces, but this would have meant missing our connection in Birmingham, so we all piled on to the busy train and fitted in where we could. A number of us chose the guards van, because we could sit down on the floor in there. I'm sure that would not be allowed today. Well, the journey was extremely slow, because the train was so overcrowded, and the time we had to transfer from Snow Hill to New Street Station in Birmingham was getting less and less. At one stop, one of the teachers managed to persuade the stationmaster to call New Street and advise them that we could be a bit late, and asked if they could hold the train for us. It was agreed that five minutes could be allowed, but not longer. As we neared Birmingham, the teachers went along the train and rounded up all the girls so that they were ready with their bags to make a dash for it. The moment that the train doors opened, we were out and instructed to follow the lead teacher, whilst one of the others counted the girls out of the train. It must have looked like a scene from St Trinian's as eighty girls, teachers and helpers rushed through the centre of Brum, struggling with luggage and looking quite unkempt after a week's camping. We made it, with a couple of minutes to spare, and were relieved to settle down for a rest in our reserved carriage, and not one girl was lost on the way.

We decided to take a trip to Devon and Cornwall, towing a caravan. Once in Cornwall, we could pay a visit to Alice's cousin Norah and her uncle Rusty, whose real name was William, but he was called Rusty, because after an accident, when he fell off a dustcart, it had affected his voice, which sounded very hoarse – hence Rusty. At the time, I was driving an old 1932 model Rover, so when we turned up to collect the caravan, the dealer had a bet with me that we would not make the journey with such an old car, so I took him on. We made steady progress and eventually arrived in Somerset. The other campers were astonished to see our old car pulling a caravan, so we made quite a stir. There was no heater in the car, so when it was cold, we wrapped ourselves in blankets. There was no aircon, of course, but if we wanted fresh air, we could open the windscreen at the bottom, to let the air in. When it rained, the wipers would only work if packed with paper, or if the passenger kept their finger on the wiper button, so we hoped that there would be no rain. The headlights were as big as dinner plates, and what a beam when they were on full!

After visiting Weston-Super-Mare, we arrived in Porlock and decided to leave the caravan there and drive over Porlock Hill, which has a gradient of 1:4 – quite a challenge for new cars, let alone my old jalopy. The old girl took it all in her stride, and we reached the top quite comfortably. On the return journey, we decided to take the toll road, for a change of route, and how surprised was the toll keeper, when we turned up. "How on earth did you get up the hill in that?" he asked, pointing to the old Rover.

"Simple," I said, "I just kept my foot to the floor."

The rest of the holiday went without incident, and the relatives were pleased to see us, though somewhat amazed by our car. After our holiday we drove home and were amused by the reaction of other road users when they saw our ancient car towing a caravan. There were lots of amazed expressions and tooting of horns. When we got back to Leicester, I returned the caravan in one piece and collected my winnings! The manager of the caravan firm paid with good grace and took a photo of the car hitched up to the caravan, to keep as a souvenir in his office. I think he was relieved that we had returned without incident.

Not long after that trip, I part-exchanged the old Rover for a Morris 8. Alice hated the old car because it looked so old-fashioned so was pleased when she saw the last of it, but it had served us well and the new car could not beat the old one for reliability. The Morris 8 was not new and needed a bit of work on the body, so instead of getting a costly re-spray, the girls set to and hand-painted it all over, a nice shade of green, which looked fine from a distance. It was only when you got too close that you could see the brush marks. Anyway, the car got us from A to B.

Thanks to the girls having pen pals, we often had visits from them in the summer, when the car was most useful taking them around the countryside. Marlene from Germany had never been to the seaside, so a trip to the East Coast was arranged. She was fascinated by the waves but was completely mystified when I mentioned that the tide was going out. "If it is going out, then why are the waves still coming in?" she asked. She thought the waves would go the other way, so I had the task of explaining the movement of the sea. I'm no scientist, but I think she understood. She may, of course, have pretended to understand, just to be polite.

Other pen friends we had were from France – Odile, Colette and Marie-Noelle (sisters), and Marja from Finland. Our two girls made reciprocal visits over the years. It is a good way to brush up language skills and to learn about different cultures. Odile thought we were rich because we had carpets, which was normal in this country but not in France. She also said, on arrival, "I drink very little wine."

Now this was in the 1950s – who drank wine in this country in those days? Certainly not working- or middle-class people. We had sweet sherry, beer or maybe Babycham, and there may have been a bottle of brandy at the back of the cupboard strictly for medicinal purposes. Our first taste of wine was probably Blue Nun!

Alice and I decided to go on a weekend trip to London, just before Christmas, to see the lights and do some shopping. We travelled on a coach from Leicester to Victoria Coach Station, because as a retired coach driver, I could get good discount on the fare. (Did someone mention busman's holiday?)

It made a nice change for someone else to be driving, and I had time to look at the scenery and some of the other drivers on the motorway. I saw lorry drivers eating their lunch, taking off jackets or sweaters whilst still moving, lighting up pipes or cigarettes, opening wrappers of sweets or chocolate bars (yes, including Yorkies), peeling a banana, shaving with an electric razor, looking at a map (before the days of satnav), fiddling with radios or tape players, etc., and all whilst hurtling along a motorway at sixty-plus mph. I will add that some car drivers were equally alarming, if not more so, considering their greater speed.

Alice was wearing a black Astrakhan coat and a beautiful white, Russian-style fur hat, which was really on trend at that time, when it was alright to wear fur.

The hat was her pride and joy. When we arrived in London, it was raining heavily, so umbrellas were needed on the short walk to our hotel. The street was crowded as we picked our way carefully along the wet pavements, trying to avoid the puddles lying there. Suddenly, a man, who was walking fairly fast, came up behind us, unnoticed, and as he passed, his umbrella somehow hooked Alice's hat off her head, and he strode on in ignorance, with the hat hanging there awaiting its fate. We rushed forward and shouted, but too late! The hat dropped into a large, dirty puddle. Alice was really upset; her beautiful hat was soaked and grubby. We hurried on to the hotel and rinsed the hat in the basin, but it was still stained. There was only one thing left to do – shampoo! Alice soaped and rinsed her hat until at last it was clean, and I went down to reception to see if I could borrow a hairdryer. The staff were highly amused when I explained why I needed one. Between the two of us we saved the hat, which came up nice and fluffy, and sparkling white. Alice thought it was a bit too fluffy, but with some careful brushing, it looked as good as new. She was glad to wear it later that evening when we went to see the lights in Oxford Street and Bond Street, because the rain had stopped and the weather suddenly turned quite cold.

Hooray for Russian hats!

Chapter Eleven
Busman Abroad

Our silver wedding was approaching, so Alice and I decided to celebrate by taking a trip to Paris. We had never been abroad before so opted for an organised tour. We travelled by coach to Lympne Airport, in Kent, ready for our first flight ever, over the Channel to Northern France, and then by coach to Paris.

We were really excited as we boarded the plane; we settled into two seats allocated to us and waited nervously for takeoff. It had rained heavily during the morning, so we were hoping to fly into better weather. The plane taxied round to the runway, revved up the engines and off we went, but as the craft pulled up into the air, a whole load of water came gushing through the roof panels, soaking both of us. Someone produced an umbrella and that is how we sat for the rest of the journey, with the umbrella up, sitting in an aeroplane. It was like a scene from a comedy show, but we didn't find it very funny at the time. We were given a free drink for our trouble, so I made sure they were doubles! The rest of the holiday went without a hitch, and we thoroughly enjoyed the sights of Paris, including a trip to the Moulin Rouge. Also because it was our silver wedding, we were given a half bottle of Champagne. Shortly after our Paris trip, Alice's father and stepmother decided that they too would like a trip abroad. Her father had been a railway man during his working life and was entitled to good discount on all rail fares, even in Europe, so they decided that a trip to Switzerland was on the books, because he had always wanted to see the mountains. Alice went as their helper, not that they needed any help, because they were both very active, but being over seventy on their first trip abroad, they lacked travel confidence, and also, the helper went at half fare.

They travelled by train to London, boarded the train to the ferry, sailed across the Channel to Calais, then boarded the sleeper which would take them down to Switzerland. Alice helped with the luggage and made sure that her parents were comfortable. They had a lovely time in Switzerland, and her father's arthritis gave him no trouble at all. He put this down to the clean mountain air. In fact, he felt so good that he took a trip on the summer Cresta run!

After a holiday in Austria, Alice and I arrived back in England, and were going through the customs hall when we were asked to go into a side room with an airline official. We were really worried and were wondering what we had done wrong, but there was no need for us to worry. It transpired that we were the fifty thousandth (or some number like it) customers to pass through the airport, and we were presented with a bottle of champagne.

In later years we went camping in Europe. The first night, we stopped off at a site in Belgium, which was situated in a disused quarry. This meant that it was quite sheltered from the wind, but we had great difficulty hammering the tent pegs into the rocky ground and so we used a couple of boulders to weigh down the tent where we couldn't fix the pegs. It rained quite a bit but, being English, we were not daunted by a spot of rain. We decided to go to the camp shop and walked along, with all three of us under the big sun umbrella which we had unpacked. I don't know what was so funny, but a Belgian woman, standing in the doorway of her chalet, called her husband to come and see the "mad English". They stood roaring with laughter at our expense, but at least we stayed dry! We just bade them a good evening, smiled and gave a royal wave as we walked by.

On the return trip we were in Belgium again, just behind the sea defences at Ostend, and it rained! It was as if the sea itself was coming over the wall on top of us. We sat in the tent playing cards, because it was too wet to venture outside, when suddenly we became aware that our feet were paddling in water – there was a river running through our tent! I went outside and saw other campers digging trenches round their tents, so I followed suit. It did the trick, so we managed to stay fairly dry that night, but the weather just got worse. We arrived at the ferry the next day, and it was still raining, and furthermore, the wind had developed overnight. We drove on to the ferry and made our way upstairs to find a seat for the voyage, and the ferry was already rolling a bit, then we set sail.

Once we were out of the harbour, we faced the full fury of a storm at sea. It was almost impossible to stand, and frantic messages came over the loudspeaker asking lorry drivers and some car owners to go down to the car deck to check on their vehicles, which were being chained down to stop them sliding about. Susan and I were hungry, but no food was being served because most of the kitchen staff were ill, and it was deemed not safe enough for them to cook anyway, so we managed with a ham sandwich. You could hear pots and pans crashing in the galley. Most passengers were lying down on the seats, Alice included. A few good sailors, like Susan and myself, wanted to go on deck for the thrill, but we were not allowed for safety reasons. In fact, it was so rough that we could not get into Dover harbour and had to sail all the way round to Tilbury in the Thames estuary, where we were sheltered from the worst of the storm. With hindsight, the ferry should never have left Ostend, because it was not long after our trip that there was the Zeebrugge disaster, when a ferry capsized, with loss of life.

Before we arrived in Ostend, we had driven through Brussels and had got completely lost, which was unusual for me, so I did the only natural thing possible: I drove into the bus station to ask for directions. A group of drivers was standing talking, and one waved me down. "You can't come here," he said sharply. "This is for buses only." I explained the situation and showed my bus drivers' licence. This immediately changed his attitude, which meant that

I was greeted as a colleague – the international brotherhood of bus drivers. They asked where I was going and told me to follow a certain bus, which would take me in the right direction for Ostend. Problem solved.

During our camping trip in France and Switzerland, we stayed in some lovely campsites and found most people very friendly and helpful. One night in France, we were having a quiet drink sitting outside our tent, when a young couple arrived to pitch camp next to us. It soon became apparent that they had never had their tent out of its bag, because they were soon arguing, not knowing how to put it all together, and it was beginning to get dark. Before our trip, we had had a dry run pitching the tent in our garden at home, and I had colour-coded each pole so that we were quite proficient in tent pitching. But this poor couple, tired after a long drive from the French coast, were near to breaking point, so I offered my services. Their tent was a smaller version of ours, and with a few tips from me, we soon had the tent erected. Alice, meanwhile, had the kettle on the stove and, when we had finished, came across with welcome cups of tea. The next morning, before we left, the young couple came to our tent with a bottle of wine as a thank-you. (I hope you are not counting the number of bottles of wine we are receiving from time to time.)

Now, I am known as a steady driver, never having a speeding ticket, so imagine my amazement, in Switzerland, when a motorcycle cop pulled to the side of me and waved me on to move faster. I was evidently going too slow and traffic was building up behind me. That is the only time I have been ordered to go faster. Whilst we were in Switzerland, we stayed at Interlaken, beside the lake. It was a stunning situation, and the weather was really hot, so Susan and I decided to take a dip in the lake where other hardy souls were swimming. We had forgotten, of course, that Swiss lakes are mainly fed by melted ice – it was so cold it took your breath away, so we didn't linger long. We were really glad of a nice cup of tea afterwards. The highlight of our holiday was a trip up the Jungfrau on the train, or, to be correct, trains. One had to change trains as you progressed up the mountain. At one point we were able to leave the train, inside the Eiger, and look out of a window cut out of the mountain side. What fabulous scenery.

As we reached the final station, up the Jungfrau, we were warned to take things very easy, because the air is very thin. We had a hot drink and sat enjoying the breathtaking scenery, watching a mountain rescue helicopter stirring up the snow as it completed a rescue exercise. Then we went for a walk, which Alice found very difficult. The high altitude was affecting her balance and she could barely stand up straight. One of the mountain rescue men walked by and asked if she was OK, then advised her to eat something if she could. She produced an apple from her bag and sat in the snow munching away. After a little while, she managed to get her mountain legs, and we walked to look at the glacier.

Nearby was a summer ski school. I had always fancied having a go at skiing, but living far away from snowy mountains, I'd never had a chance until now. Susan and I decided to have a go, and Alice would film us with Susan's cine camera. We spent a jolly hour skiing, and we were getting on quite well for beginners, and we certainly enjoyed it, but then it was time to get the return train. As we walked back to the station, I began to feel a little unwell. The train was crowded, so we had to stand, but I felt really ill and collapsed down onto the floor. The people around us were very helpful and offered drinks and a seat. I evidently looked very grey, and certainly felt very grey. As the train moved slowly down the mountain side, I began to feel better, and by the time we reached Interlaken, I was just about back to my normal self – I had just overdone the exercise at high altitude. Another lesson learned. Still, I had proof of my skiing exploits on film, except, when we saw the printed film, Alice had held the camera upside down!

In later years, we went on holiday with our daughter Ann and her husband, so that we could babysit for our grandson, whilst they were performing in cabaret in the hotel. Because they had late nights, we looked after the little lad in the mornings, and he slept in our room at night so that we could keep an eye on him.

One year, we went to Portugal, so that Ann could do the cabaret for New Year's Eve. In Portugal, all the locals, including young children, go out on the town to celebrate, but we decided to stay in with our grandson. The hotel manager was surprised that we didn't want to go out and join in the fun, so to make up for our "loss", he gave me the key to the bar, with the strict instructions that we help ourselves to anything we fancied to drink, free of charge. I certainly enjoyed a glass or two of malt whisky that night!

Chapter Twelve
What Was Life Before the Bus?

When I was fourteen, I was apprenticed to a car mechanic, because my schoolwork was considered under par, and I showed an aptitude for things technical. However, the apprenticeship did not last long, because the firm I was with folded and I was out of useful employment. The upside was that during the time I was there, I learned to drive.

One did not have to take a driving test in those days, but then there was little traffic. I tried out various unskilled jobs, just to make some small income, but nothing inspired me. I often wonder why nobody suggested following my father's footsteps into the jewellery trade, because I had quite an artistic side to me, but that wasn't to be.

My father, who used to maintain the clocks in the big houses in Lincoln, heard that one of the households was looking for a chauffeur. An interview was arranged, and in spite of my tender years, I got the job. My starting wage was around ten shillings (50p) a week, with uniform and bed and board provided. I was expected to do other tasks as well as driving and car maintenance, such as cleaning the house windows, sweeping the yard or pavement, carrying messages around the town or any other jobs the butler could find to keep me busy.

It was whilst I was working as a chauffeur that I first caught sight of a pretty young parlour maid who worked in the house next door. Her name was Alice. I often had to deliver messages to the house next door and always accepted the cook's offer of a cup of tea, in the hope that I could catch sight of Alice. Looking back, I think that the cook was something of a matchmaker. Anyway, somehow I managed to persuade Alice to walk out with me. I felt so proud to have Alice beside me. She was very pretty and stylish, and she was once runner-up in a beauty queen competition run by the *Lincolnshire Echo*. Well, romance blossomed, and we started courting. Alice was made up to the position of Lady's Maid. She was so highly thought of that her lady let her choose her own uniform, which was royal blue instead of the usual black.

When the families in the big houses went away on holiday, then the staff had some fun. The families were away for about six weeks in France or Italy, and they hired staff where they were staying. We usually had a two-week break at this time, when the house was closed up, with dust sheets everywhere. Following the break, we had about a month to give the house a thorough clean – all hands on deck – including the butler. That is when we got up to mischief.

My master had a collapsible opera hat for visits to the theatre in London. We decided to "have a go" with it. I removed the hat from its case – it looked very smooth, shiny and expensive. We all tried it on and had a good laugh. Our master must have had a large head, because the hat swamped most of us, especially the young scullery maid – it covered her head completely. Then some bright spark decided to collapse it down. (For once it wasn't me.) With a click, the hat snapped flat. We'd all seen actors at the cinema tap open their hat, so how difficult would it be? We tried everything – it would not budge! We had to wait for the butler to come home from the pub to put it right. He gave us a heated dressing-down, but as he turned to go to his pantry, did I spot the beginnings of a little smile on his face?

In Alice's big house, there was a musical toilet tissue dispenser, which played a little tune from a selection of four, when activated by the action of pulling the tissue. Why anyone would want such a strange object is beyond me, but we tried it out anyway. The tune "Oh I Do Like to Be Beside the Seaside" played and played and *played*! No matter what we tried it would not stop! What to do? The family were due back later that day, and we could not possibly let them be greeted by a fanfare from the lavatory. We'd all be in trouble. I dashed round to the garage next door, grabbed my tool kit and set to work opening up the device, fiddling about a bit until it stopped. Phew! I carefully replaced the back, rubbed it clean of fingerprints and dirty marks, and hurried back to my place next door. The dulcet tones of the musical toilet tissue dispenser were, as far as I know, never heard again. (Nobody could figure out why.)

When I worked as a chauffeur, I remember one night vividly. I was driving my employer home after a dinner engagement. It was very late, and he was sitting in the passenger seat beside me, as was his wont when it was just the two of us. (He liked to keep an eye on things.) The road was deserted, apart from us. Suddenly, ahead of us, we could see a cyclist in the middle of the road, well illuminated by our powerful headlights. "It's a bit lonely out here to be cycling. It's a wonder he can see where he is going," said my employer. As we drove closer, the cyclist suddenly disappeared! "Stop the car!" cried my boss. I pulled up sharpish, and we both got out of the car. We looked around, but there was no sign of the cyclist. There was no turning, no ditch, no gateway, no bridge, no wall, no fence, no tree. There was absolutely nowhere he could have hidden or fallen. I looked at my employer; he looked at me and said, in a very quiet voice, "Taylor, I think we had better get away from here." I couldn't have agreed more.

Now for something a little lighter.

On our days off, Alice and I would sometimes cycle to her parents' house, which was about six miles from Lincoln. On one such trip, her father had recently mown his front lawn, and so there was a pile of grass cuttings waiting to be composted. We thought that we could have a bit of fun with these. We gathered a pile of cuttings and made them up into a neat parcel tied up with string. We walked to the main road, placed the parcel beside the road and hid behind a hedge to see what happened. Shortly afterwards, a couple of cyclists came along and looked briefly at the parcel but went on their way. After about ten minutes, we could hear a car coming. The car stopped next to the parcel, the driver got out, looked around, then quickly climbed back in the car with the parcel, with a big smile upon his face. I wonder what treasure he thought he'd found? Meanwhile, we were doubled up with silent laughter behind the hedge.

Alice's Story About a Battery

On a visit home, my father was wondering how to dispose of a radio battery. In those days, wireless sets worked with huge batteries and once they were dead, they were very difficult to dispose of. Living in the country, we got rid of our waste by burying, burning, composting or re-using – no bin men for us. So, how to get rid of this cumbersome battery? It could not be treated like our normal rubbish. Then someone had a bright idea. Why not wrap it up like we did with the grass cuttings? So this was done, and we wheelbarrowed it down to the main road and left it beside the grass verge and went home. Who should cycle along a short time later but Percy? He picked up the neatly packed, heavy parcel, balanced it on his handlebars and brought it home to us. So we had to try again. We traipsed down the road once more and left it in the same place and returned home. Percy had a lot of ribbing. How could he fall for such a trick after the grass-cuttings incident? He had a good laugh about it later as it was all part of the fun.

Later that day, the local AA man came along on his motorbike and stopped to look at the parcel. We had overlooked the fact that the wrapping paper we used had been used before, and no-one had noticed my father's name and address in one corner. On seeing this, the AA man thought that my father had lost a parcel, so he kindly delivered it to the local railway signal box where he knew that my father worked. My father found some old paper in the waiting room, re-wrapped the parcel, making sure that there were no clues to ownership, and put it on the next train to Lincoln.

What a surprise for someone!

Alf's Car

Much of my life revolved around transport, be it bus, bicycle or car, but on one occasion it was Alfred's car, not mine, which caused a stir. Alice, the girls and I were visiting my parents in their house overlooking West Common when the telephone rang. It was my brother Alfred ringing to say that he was in Lincoln at the engineering works, and he would come and visit once he had finished his meeting and had refuelled his car. Sometime later, we were in the front garden with Pa, examining the holly bush, when we heard a strange mechanical sound coming closer. Seconds later, Alfred's car appeared in thick cloud of acrid, stinking smoke and pulled up at the road gate. (It was a private gated road at the time.) Pa told me to fetch a bucket of water, because he thought that the car might burst into flames at any moment, whilst he opened the gate. Alfred pulled up on the opposite side of the road, away from the houses, and jumped out. Gradually the smoke subsided, so my bucket of water was not needed.

Alfred then explained what had happened. He had gone to the garage to fill his car up before his trip back to Corby, where he worked as a crane engineer at the steel works. The mechanic at the garage said that the pumps were out of action, but he had managed to stockpile a few cans of petrol before that. He told Alfred that he would sell him one red can of petrol. Alfred paid up, and the mechanic went back to the office without further conversation. Alfred picked up the green can and emptied it into his tank.

Unfortunately, Alfred had a very poor sense of smell, and could not differentiate between the smell of petrol and paraffin! Yes, he had topped his car up with paraffin (green can) instead of petrol (red can) and had not noticed until he came to start his car. The smoke and the noise told him something was wrong, and the mechanic came running. He gave Alfred two options – one: siphon the tank or two: just fill the tank with a couple of cans of petrol to dilute the paraffin. Alfred opted for the second option, because it was quicker. So off he set with smoke billowing and engine grinding. I was amazed that the car actually managed to move at all. The smell of paraffin lingered for weeks, and nobody let him forget it, especially brother Jim and me.

On another occasion, it was Susan who helped Alfred to fix his car. It began to play up, so Alfred parked outside Ma and Pa's house and lifted the bonnet to see what he could do. As I said before, Alfred was an engineer so knew quite a bit about engines, but this time he was having difficulty. Susan was on the path playing with her skipping rope but was keen to look under the bonnet, because she always seemed interested in how things work. Alfred was telling Susan the names of different parts of the engine when he yelled out – he had just had a shock from something he touched. It was at this point that I came out to offer any help that I could; after all, I had spent some time as an apprentice mechanic and knew something about bus engines. Time went by, and we were getting nowhere. Pa's neighbour, Major Armstrong, who had served with Lawrence in Arabia, came out to offer his advice. We stood around the car discussing the situation, until the small voice of Susan was heard to say, "Uncle Alfred, is it anything to do with the shock?" Alfred had a brief rolling of eyes heavenward, called himself an idiot and in no time at all had fixed the problem. He had completely forgotten about the shock, but it obviously had an impact on Susan. Well done, Susan, you saved the day.

In later years, when the girls had their own cars, I showed them how to do simple car maintenance like checking the oil and water, how to change a wheel or check tyre pressures and inflate tyres. I used to accompany them when they had their L plates on. Both were quite confident and passed their tests first time. When Ann was learning, I gave her the instruction to turn right at the next turning, but we ended up in a pub yard because she mistook the entrance to the pub for the road. It was a good job it was not opening time, so there were no cars parked and no damage done. When Susan was learning, she used to drive us to Lincoln most weekends to visit family. I would be in the passenger seat, supposedly keeping an eye on her as a learner, but frequently I would nod off, completely relaxed. Well done Ann and Susan!

Tramp – an Incident Never Forgotten

This story has nothing to do with transport, but it left a memory. One morning, I was walking through the market when I saw the local "character" shuffling along between the stalls. He was what one would call a tramp, having no fixed abode, and he was very unkempt and grubby. He was known as Old Jess to everyone who was aware of him, but nobody knew much about him, except that it was thought that he had been in the military. He slept rough, perhaps in a barn or shed if he was lucky, or more often under a hedge or on a bench. He evidently could not bear to be confined, probably due to some trauma he had suffered. The police left him alone because he was never any trouble. He frequented the market, because a few kind stallholders would give him a little food, which he called a "kindness", and in return he would give them thanks and a blessing. It was the only time he spoke. Mainly, he kept himself isolated but could be seen around the town on occasion. He used to wash himself in the river but wore the same filthy, ragged clothes, unless some kind person gave him some old cast-offs.

Well, as I said, I saw him as I was walking through the market. Just in front of him was a lady carrying a basket full of eggs, but she suddenly missed her footing on the uneven pavement and fell over, scattering the eggs. Whilst people tried to help the lady, Old Jess picked up her basket, very carefully replaced any unbroken eggs and quietly handed the basket to the grateful lady. He refused the sixpence she offered him, and she watched in amazement as he bent down, scooped the spilled egg whites and yolks in his hand, using a piece of shell, and proceeded to eat them straight off the pavement. When things are not going too well for me, I often think about Old Jess – he seemed to have all he wanted, even though that was very little, and he had an inner calm that is often missing in people in today's busy world. I never saw him again.

Chapter Thirteen
Alice's Tale

Alice with big sister Flo and twins – Rose and Lily

Percy's Bus

When I was a girl, I used to go to Sunday school with my sisters, Flo, Rose and Lily. We wore our best clothes, complete with straw bonnet. We usually cut across the fields, unless, of course, it was too wet, then that meant a long trek round by road.

On this particular day it was fine, and we had gone through the first field and were making our way through the second one, where there was a herd of cows grazing. As we went along, we kept our eyes focussed on the ground on the lookout for cow pats, because it really would not be nice to turn up at church with stinking shoes. I was concentrating so hard on looking for cow pats that I didn't realise how close I was to the rear end of a beast who, at the moment I was passing by, decided to evacuate her bowels with explosive force all over me! My sisters all burst out laughing seeing my plight, but only Lily opted to escort me home, at a distance! I fought back the tears. This thick, stinking, warm, brown mess was all over me. My best dress, my hat, my face, my shoes, my hair – everywhere. It was revolting, sickening, disgusting and any other words you can think of. I was just hoping and praying that I was not seen by any of my school friends, because they would have a great time teasing me and making jokes at my expense, but not with malice, I must add. That's what friends do – good-humoured "joshing".

Mother was shocked to see the state I was in and immediately set to work stripping me off in the yard and putting me under the pump – it was freezing! Can you imagine it, being sluiced down with cold, high-pressure pump water? Lily helped by running to fetch a large towel from the kitchen, and in no time at all, I was wrapped in a blanket, sitting in front of the warm range, drinking hot milk and honey. I'm not sure, but I think there may well have been a touch of brandy in the mug too.

Poor Mother had the unpleasant task of washing my clothes, but as usual, she did a brilliant job and did her best to mask the lingering smell of cow poo by using sweet-smelling herbs in the final rinse. I was glad when I grew out of those clothes, because I was sure there was always a faint whiff of dung on a warm day. Unfortunately for Lily, she had those clothes as hand-me-downs, because Rose was too big. (She never complained.)

My father was highly amused when he heard about my mishap and in later years would often say, "No wonder you grew so tall, Peg, it was that good fertiliser when you were young." (He called me Peg because of my long legs, and I could run very fast.) Just think what city kids were missing.

Being able to run fast helped me out of several situations when I was young. One day, I was walking home from school with the twins, Rose and Lily, when we came across a large, stinking, dead fish in a dry ditch. How it got there was anybody's guess. We were curious, so we started poking it with sticks we had found, only to discover that it was absolutely full of maggots. As we stood there prodding and poking, Arthur Simmons, the class bully, came along and demanded to know what we were doing. He pushed us roughly to one side and bent over to get a better look. At that moment, I saw red and gave him a huge push, and he toppled into the ditch, face first onto the maggots. He got up quickly and, to our amazement, started to cry – not just a whimper, but a real wide-mouthed bellow, just like a two-year-old. Arthur Simmons, the bully, was *crying*! "Crybaby, crybaby," we chorused, and then fled as fast as we could. After that, we never had trouble from him again, because we only had to say, "*Fish!*", and he would leave us alone.

Something that happened to my mother: she was cycling home one afternoon, when a youth, leaning on a field gate, called out to her, "Hey up, Missus, your back wheel's going round!" She was somewhat startled and turned her head to look down at the wheel to see what was wrong. She overbalanced and went sprawling on to the road. The youth ran off laughing, and my mother picked herself up, realising, with huge embarrassment, that she had fallen for one of the oldest tricks around. Luckily she only suffered a few bruises and damaged pride.

Her pride was dented on another occasion too. She was walking along the lane, heading for the main road, where she could catch the weekly bus to market, and she was carrying a heavy basket full of apples and jars of honey to sell. One of the local farmhands pulled up in his donkey cart. "Would you like a lift, Missus?" he asked.

"I don't mind if I do," my mother replied.

"Well," said the man, "if you don't mind, then neither do I. Gee up!" Off he went to market, leaving Mother standing on the roadside, somewhat stunned, but lesson learned... Say what you mean!

My poor mother had a cleft palate, which meant that she could not sound some of her words properly, especially any word with an S. Unfortunately, her surname was Smith, and her address had three S words, which sometimes made life a little difficult. She always carried a card with her in case she had to give her name and address to anyone. The family could all understand her perfectly well, because we were used to her way of speaking. I expect nowadays she would have surgery to correct the problem.

My father was always busy in our huge garden. He grew a good variety of fruit and vegetables. We never bought fruit or vegetables, because there was a system of bartering with neighbours. No-one went without food in the village, because if someone met hard times, we all helped by donating "surplus" food. There was never any surplus food, just neighbours helping out someone in need. He also kept up to fifty chickens, one or two pigs and three or four beehives. He encouraged us to talk quietly to the bees and reassure them that we were there to look after them. We four girls never got stung by bees. Mother, on the other hand, never went near the bees, because they did not seem to like her and she occasionally got stung. Were they jealous? Who knows?

Honey harvest was the best of times – I absolutely adore fresh honeycomb and always asked the bees' permission to taste some. Pure liquid gold! Even to this day, I only have to see a piece of comb in a jar, or even just a picture of honeycomb, and my mouth starts to water. The strange thing is – I really don't have a sweet tooth, but it is such a strong memory of my childhood. I had two very serious illnesses when I was young – rheumatic fever and pneumonia.

Alice's Tale

Alice's parents, Jane and James Smith

With the latter, I was so ill that they were saying prayers for me in church, and the vicar came several times to the house to pray over me. Penicillin was not yet available, so my mother resorted to an ancient country recipe to keep me alive. Warm milk and honey, or more often, hot lemon, rum and honey. This liquid was spooned into me at regular intervals, and I survived. Thank goodness for *honey*! I still use these recipes today for coughs and colds.

One day at the end of the garden, Father was scything some nettles which had sprung up around the open cesspit. (We had no sewers in those days, out in the country.) Suddenly, he sneezed so violently and unexpectedly that his false teeth shot out of his mouth and landed with a plop into the stinking pit. He lay down his scythe, rolled up his sleeve, plunged his arm into the slime and started to feel around for his teeth. He was in luck, because the slurry was fairly thick, so the teeth had not sunk too low. When he retrieved his precious dentures he went up to the yard, swilled them and his arm under the pump, then popped the teeth back into his mouth. He must have seen the amazed look on my face because he turned to me and said, "Don't worry, Peg, we all have to swallow a peck of muck before we kick the bucket." Well, it didn't seem to do him any harm because he was never ill, and in his seventies he could amuse his grandchildren by standing on his head! He was not a man to sit still for long. After a full day working in the signal box, he would change his clothes, eat his dinner and then disappear into the garden until the light faded, never mind the weather. He'd be planting, pruning, weeding, mowing, digging and harvesting. When it came to the gathering, he used to encourage all of us to join in. His work didn't stop at home either. If someone had an unwanted swarm of bees on their property, they would call for my father, who was only too glad to take such a valuable asset home. He was usually paid in kind, perhaps a homemade cheese or a bottle of elderberry wine.

Sometimes he would be called upon to build a well for someone. My father was a water diviner, and he would take his special hazel twig to dowse for water and, once located, would start to dig. Sometimes he was paid cash for this service and sometimes in goods. (Perhaps a pheasant in season.)

His divining skills always fascinated me, and I tried many times to make the stick work, but it was not to be. My daughters did not inherit the skill either.

I think I mentioned before, we always had plenty of food on the table. Apart from home-grown fruit and veg we had home-reared chicken and pork, and if we had no animals ready to slaughter, father would shoot crow, rook or pigeon for pies. In season there would be pheasant, duck and rabbit. I will add, that game was taken with the landowners' permission, not by poaching!

When it came to slaughtering the pig, neighbours all joined in. They took it in turns to kill a pig so that meat could be shared around. On the allotted day, the children were dispatched to gather field mushrooms or hedgerow fruit such as blackberries, rosehips and elderberries, or watercress from the stream, depending on the season. By the time we had filled the collection basket and returned home, there would be no sign of the slaughter, except for the wet yard which had recently been sluiced down to get rid of the blood. Some of the blood was used to make black pudding – now that is something I cannot stomach.

There is an old country saying, "Every part of the pig is used, except the grunt." How true. The pig's head was traditionally given to the owner, and this would be cooked in the copper in the wash house. The rest of the meat was shared out, even the tail. This would be popped in the stock pot which simmered on the range, then later given to the dog to chew. The house would smell of bacon for weeks to come as the cured hock was suspended from a hook in the ceiling in the kitchen, waiting to be carved when ready. A sticky fly-catching paper was always hung nearby to try and stop flies from settling on the meat – it seemed to work. I never liked to see the little black remains of flies hanging there, so I tried not to look. I was always glad when a new paper was hung up and the old one thrown on the fire. We country kids accepted the slaughter of animals as part of life. It was either that or go hungry.

During the war, when meat was rationed, people had to have a permit to keep a pig. Everyone in the village who kept a pig complied with this ruling and had the appropriate permit, but what was not broadcast was the fact that many people had a secret pig which they kept hidden until it was time to slaughter. This extra animal helped to keep people fed during a very difficult time.

When I was young, it was normal for country folk to travel by horse and cart, or some sort of wagon pulled by donkey, pony or even dog. Rural public transport was more or less non-existent, except for the one bus a week to and from Lincoln market. There were, of course, trains for longer journeys, but most people resorted to cycling or walking. My father managed to save enough to buy a motorbike and sidecar to ferry us around to visit various relatives, or perhaps a rare visit to the seaside. For those trips we usually travelled by train, and because father worked for the railways, he got free travel for him and discount for his family.

When we went out on the motorbike, Father would be driving, with big sister Flo riding pillion. Mother, who would never ride pillion, sat in the front seat of the sidecar with one of the twins on her knee, and I squeezed into the tiny rear seat with the other twin either on my knee or squeezed in beside me. Eventually, we became too big to continue with this arrangement, and I was getting fed up with the twins being sick on me – they didn't travel well. So father bought an old Ford car. In later years we would fit ten people into the car – Mother, Father, sister Rose with her four children, and me with my two. Mother sat in the front seat with the youngest on her knee, Rose and me in the back with the remaining five children either on our knees, squashed in between or sitting on cushions on the floor. What an adventure. No health and safety in those days, and we came to no harm. Of course, there was very little traffic in those days.

In the meantime, back to the subject of pony carts. One day, our cousin Bill called in to see us on his way back from market. He had bought a new pony and cart, and he thought it would be a nice gesture to give us a ride in it to his home and back, just a few miles away. Besides, he wanted to show it off. There were several bales of hay which he had bought for fodder, so we sat on those. It was a lovely day, and the four of us were singing happily, when we came to an abrupt halt.

We were about to cross over a white-painted wooden bridge, when the pony took fright and refused to budge. Instead, it began to back away from the bridge, onto the grass verge at the side of the road, towards the ditch. We were hanging on for dear life, and Bill was trying his best to stop the pony, but to no avail. It backed over the edge and plummeted down into the muddy ditch, and we ended up in a pile of children and straw bales at the end of the cart, a bit bruised but not really hurt. The pony, meanwhile, was dangling about six foot in the air, still fastened to the shafts of the cart, whinnying very loudly and flailing around with his legs. We kids found this sight very amusing and could not help ourselves for laughing.

Luckily for us, the local vicar came along on his bicycle and, doing a bad job of disguising his mirth, went and sought help from the nearby farm. A group of burly farm workers soon dragged the wagon out of the ditch, and after checking that everyone and the pony was OK, we were on our way home, looking very grubby. Word soon spread amongst the farming community and Bill never lived it down.

My father used to tell the tale of when he was cycling home from work and his stomach was very uncomfortable. It suddenly got so bad that he needed a lavatory urgently, but he was in the middle of nowhere, so he did what any country man would do in the circumstances. He laid his bike on the grass verge and climbed over the nearby gate into what he thought was an empty meadow, surrounded by a thick hawthorn hedge, and lowered his trousers. What a relief – but that was short-lived. He could hear and feel a thudding sound. He looked over his shoulder and could see a huge bull charging towards him. He struggled to the gate with his trousers still at half-mast and threw himself over the gate, hoping that the bull would not crash through or jump over the gate. Yes, bulls can jump! Luckily for him the bull stopped his charge once my father was out of sight.

Another lesson learned – look before you ****.

Whilst in the lavatory area, another story comes to mind regarding my father. We were visiting my grandparents who lived in a small cottage with no gas or electricity, and no running water – therefore, no flushing lavatory. The toilet facilities were very basic: a wooden hut at the end of the garden, with a pit underneath. This pit would be cleared out occasionally by the council pit men. The seat was a plank of wood with a hole cut in it, and the tissue was a pile of old newspapers. Sometimes, the newspapers would be torn into rough squares and threaded on a string, which would then be hung on a hook nearby. The paper was quite scratchy, but a quick scrunching/rubbing action softened it up a little. There was usually a bucket containing sand, soil or ash which could be scattered onto the contents of the pit, to try and mask the smell a little and to keep the flies at bay. It didn't work!

Anyway, during our visit, my father needed to use the facilities and was sitting in quiet contemplation, when he heard a loud clucking coming from the pit beneath him. My grandmother had a pet chicken which was blind, and it was always getting into scrapes. This time it had fallen into the pit. Well, it was a free-range chicken! My father rescued the poor fowl, took it up to the pump in the yard and, to an accompaniment of terrible squawking, gave it a good sluice down until it looked clean. I don't think that chicken ever graced the table.

Percy's Puns – oh, no!

Q. Why did the chicken use the pelican crossing?
A. Because there is no such thing as a chicken crossing!

Q. What do you call a stand-up chicken?
A. A comedi-hen.

Q. Why did the rubber chicken cross the road?
A. She wanted to stretch her legs. (Oh, no.)

Q. Why did the dressed-up chicken cross the road?
A. She was going to a hen party. (Please stop!)

Just one more:

Q. If a white hen lays white eggs and a brown hen lays brown eggs, what colour eggs does a black rooster lay?
A. It would be a miracle if *he* laid any!

My father had an unusual sense of humour, which is why I think he got on well with Percy. Mind you, when he first met Percy, it was a different matter. After his first visit to meet my parents, my father said to me, "You needn't bring that pug-nosed b***** here again!" However, my mother liked Percy and put in a good word for him with my father. So, after a few visits, once he got to know Percy, everything turned out well.

The next incident I recall occurred when we were visiting my parents. I was helping to do the washing-up in the scullery after breakfast. I had given Susan a bacon rind to chew on as she went out in the garden to see her granddad. (She loved the fat on bacon rind.) He was busy digging the soil, which revealed a very large earthworm. He knew how much I hated things that wriggle, especially worms. I'm fine with spiders and beetles, etc. But worms – no thank you. He picked up the juicy worm, handed it to Susan, replacing the bacon rind, and said, "Go and give this to your mum." So off she went to the scullery, with the worm squirming in her tight fist, and plonked it on the draining board and said, "Granddad told me to give you this." I nearly passed out. I hate worms, and I thought for a moment that Susan had been chewing a worm instead of the bacon rind. It was then I caught a glimpse of my father peeping round the corner of the washhouse, with an enormous grin on his face.

It is no wonder that the girls enjoyed visiting. He loved to tell them about things growing in the garden and would often give them a taste of something they didn't see very often, like fennel, dill, redcurrants and gooseberries. It would amuse him if the fruits were not quite ripe and were sour, then the girls would pull faces whilst he had a chuckle to himself.

He let them gather the eggs from the chicken coop. To amuse them further, he would tell them tales or he would stand on his head, even though he was in his seventies. He also perfected the trick of finding a penny behind your ear.

I never did work that one out.

In the early days of the Second World War, my father was working as stationmaster and signalman. This was normally the work of two men, but there was a shortage of able-bodied men, so my father did both jobs.

It was during a stint as stationmaster that he was approached by a young couple with a tiny babe in arms. They had escaped from Poland with their baby daughter but were unable to bring their older daughter, who was staying with grandparents whilst the baby was born. They had very little luggage because they had fled in haste to escape Nazi persecution, and as a chemical engineer, Victor did not wish to be made to work for the Nazi war machine, producing chemical weapons. Anna, Victor and baby Barbara had made their way across Europe and had somehow found their way to this small station down the line from Lincoln.

They were desperate to find somewhere to stay and asked my father if he knew of anywhere they could go, for very little rent. They had a little money with them, but Victor said he would work to pay for food and lodging. He said it was his duty to provide for his family.

My father was somewhat taken with this young couple and was very sympathetic to their situation; also, he admired their bravery. He bid them sit in the waiting room until he finished his shift, gave them cups of tea and said he would sort something out for them.

After a couple of hours, my father finished work; he collected his cycle and Anna, Victor and the baby, and escorted them to his house. He spoke briefly to my mother, who immediately agreed with my father that they should stay with them, as they had a spare room. Anna and Vic were overwhelmed. Mother gave them clean linen and towels, and in no time at all, they were settled in.

Victor asked Father if he knew of any work available locally because he wanted to pay his way. Luckily, Father knew most of the local farmers who were short of workers, due to the war, so within days Vic was earning enough money to pay a small rent and something towards food.

The latter was not really necessary, because as I said before, my family were self-sufficient with food. Vic also liked to help Father in the garden. The refugees became part of the family, and Barbara was a playmate for Susan when we visited, being a similar age. Likewise, a couple of my sister Rose's children were also similarly aged and would take Barbara under their wings.

I mentioned earlier that Vic was a chemical engineer, but he could not get a job in that field during the war, because he was a foreign national. Vic, Anna and Barbara (commonly known as Basha) stayed with my parents for several years until the war ended, then they took British Nationality and Vic got a good job in the chemical engineering industry, near Manchester.

A few years after the war, Vic managed to trace his other daughter whom they had had to leave behind in order to escape. She was safe and well living with her grandparents in a very remote area of Poland. They were able to bring her to Britain to join her close family. They kept in touch right up to my father's death in 1962, and they always thanked him greatly for helping them and for giving them hope.

Chapter Fourteen
Highland Bus

My first trip to Scotland was a bit of a worry, because I had never been there before. I bought books and maps, and studied them very carefully, but due to a misprint of a road number on my itinerary, I got a bit lost in Stirling. Through the onboard microphone I was telling the passengers about the Wallace Memorial, when I took a wrong turning, then came along the same bit of road, saying again, "And on the left, the Wallace Memorial." So I tried again, but succeeded in taking the same road again, and as we passed, there was a chorus from the back of the coach: "And on the left, the Wallace Memorial!" I didn't live it down that week.

I made many journeys up to the Isle of Skye. This was a popular nine-day tour from Leicester, and it was always fully booked. On the way, we travelled through some of the most spectacular scenery in the British Isles, especially Glen Shiel, which is as wild and remote as any place in Scotland, but not so much fun for me driving along fifty-four miles of single track road, in a huge coach, with only limited passing places. There was one place which was very difficult, where it was bottom gear all the way up the mountainside, with a narrow bridge set at an angle to the road. It was not bad for a car to negotiate, but in the coach, there were about two inches each side, so I had to get it right first time. Luckily, years of experience stood me in good stead. However, once at the top, the view was breathtaking – well worth the effort.

Highland Bus

I had a small adventure on one trip, when the Scottish authorities decided to repair the road. They planted charges by the road and blew it up, to widen it, so when I arrived, there was no road at all alongside Loch Logne, so I pulled up and asked one of the roadmen in a yellow safety helmet which direction I should take. He proceeded to direct me over several piles of rubble, nearly tipping me into the loch, until I reached terra firma. I am told that there is now a good road all around the Kyle of Lochalsh.

On the return journey, we used to stop for lunch at the St Enoch Station Hotel in Glasgow. Here we had parking problems, but it was arranged that on arrival, we were directed by the police to take the coach into the station via the exit archway – the only way we could get in – then park on platform 9. There was just enough room to turn the coach round between platforms 8 and 9, after the passengers had alighted on the forecourt. The procedure was to open a large iron gate, drive through and close the gate between the two ticket collectors' barriers. One day, I had arrived early, parked my coach, had my lunch and still had half an hour to spare before the passengers were due back, so I returned to the coach park and stood leaning on the gate watching the world go by. There was only one ticket collector on duty on platform 9 when a packed train pulled in. Suddenly, someone tapped me on the shoulder. It was a young lady with two children and a pushchair. "May I come through here, please?" she asked, mistaking me for a collector, in my navy suit. She handed me her ticket and was quickly followed by about two hundred other passengers, who had broken away from the slow-moving official queue nearby. I finished up with a stack of tickets in my hand and was a bit worried about what the collector would say. Luckily, he smiled and said, "Thanks, you've done a grand job there, laddie."

I should have mentioned before that when turning the coach round on the platforms, one had to drive the coach with the front almost touching any train waiting there. One day, a man sat watching me through the carriage window. He got up and walked to the open door and shouted, "You'll never get that thing in here!"

On another trip to Skye, I had a group of six young ladies amongst the passengers, which was quite unusual, because most of our customers were middle-aged or retired couples. Well, these six young ladies were quite charming and were well liked by their fellow passengers. During the tour, we stayed for one night at a very old hotel where most of the bedrooms had four-poster beds and the lounges were dark-panelled, with stags' heads, swords and shields, and even a couple of suits of armour for decoration – just the place for a ghost or two – as one of the girls remarked.

Later that evening, five of the girls came to see me and asked if I would mind being a ghost, just for fun. I'm always up for a laugh, so I agreed. The sixth girl in the group, Mary, had gone to bed early to read her book. They led me to the corridor where Mary's room was situated, draped a sheet over my head and retreated to a safe distance to watch. I stood making suitable ghostly noises and waved my arms about. Mary's door opened, and after a brief pause she said, "What do you want, Percy?" I was never very good at acting, apart from acting the goat.

In those days, locks and bolts were a secondary consideration on the Isle of Skye, so it came as no surprise to find that there were no locks on any of the room doors in the hotel where we were staying. People were so honest, locks were deemed unnecessary, but that was not always the case, as I soon found out.

It was around this time that my youngest daughter, who was studying geography at college, had an interest in geology and liked to collect interesting rock samples. So, on my travels, I picked up a variety of stones for her collection. Now, not far from the hotel was a lovely pebble beach, so I strolled down there one evening to collect a few interesting specimens, unaware that six pairs of eyes were watching my every move. I filled my pockets and sauntered back to the hotel for a nightcap in the bar. I was usually the last person to retire, as I had to be on duty to make sure the customers were all happy and comfortable. At last I was free to retire and made my way into my room, then saw at once that there was something wrong with my bed – it was sagging in the middle! Lifting the cover, I found a dozen enormous boulders neatly tied with a bow of toilet paper! It took me ages to carry the stones downstairs, with a little help from the barman, who wasn't much use, with tears of laughter rolling down his cheeks. No prizes for guessing the culprits. It amazed me how no-one saw the girls carrying those huge stones into the hotel, or perhaps they had inside help. Having disposed of the rockery, I had a quick wash and tried to put on my pyjamas – they were very neatly stitched up – just like me!

One would not expect to see many gardens on the Isle of Skye, due to the climate, but at a little place called Duisdale there was the most perfect vegetable garden I have ever seen, even outshining that of my father-in-law, in fertile Lincolnshire. It covered about an acre, with everything growing in luxurious perfect rows. I asked the gardener his secret, but his reply was, "Nae secret, laddie, just patience and hard work."

It was on another Skye trip that I had a spot of trouble with the coach. After leaving Glasgow, the rear suspension collapsed, so having phoned the depot, I was instructed to nurse it as far as Carlisle, where we had an overnight stop, and they would try and get a replacement coach to me as soon as possible. I struggled on at about fifteen mph, hoping that the motorists stuck behind me on the old A74 would forgive me for holding them up. They must have thought I was crazy, driving so slowly. However, I did stop in lay-bys as often as I could, to let them pass, so we were about two hours late reaching our hotel, but they were very understanding and had kept a meal for us. Not one of my customers complained.

I left the coach at the local depot, ready for the relief driver to collect. The next morning, I set off early to collect the relief coach from the depot, but it wasn't there, nor was the coach I had brought in the night before.

"Your man has taken your coach," said the depot foreman.

"Where's the new one then?" I asked.

"It's not here," was his obvious reply. As I walked back to the hotel wondering what to do, I passed the town bus station and there, at the front, was a coach. There was nobody about, so, presuming that this was meant for me, I took out my key, climbed in and drove back to the hotel.

Inside our coaches was a large mirror for the driver's use, to enable him to see the rear window, but if it was carefully adjusted, one could keep an eye on the passengers as well. It was on a seven-day cruise that I had twenty-five passengers, including three singles. The rest were married couples – quite a nice party. It usually took me a couple of days to sort them out or try to guess who would be good for a drawing-room story. The three singles were two ladies, one young (Betty), one middle-aged (Madam) and one young man whom I shall call Jack. As we continued the tour, I noticed that the young couple had a lot in common and, at my suggestion, were able to sit together on the coach, as there were a few vacant seats. Not only that, but I suggested to the head waiter at each hotel we visited that it would be a good deed if a table was reserved, unofficially, for Jack and Betty, and I would give the nod when they came in for their meal. I was beginning to enjoy playing cupid.

Now, Madam, who was the odd one out in the party, had a habit of butting into other people's conversations, and she forced her attention onto others when it was not really wanted. I could fully understand her position, being alone, but she was becoming a complete bore, which was a shame, because the other passengers had really tried to include her in things. One night, the manager asked me to ensure that everyone was in early for dinner, because he had arranged a party in the lounge afterwards. So after dinner, we all assembled for the party – my party of twenty-five and six American tourists. Each of us was asked to do a turn to entertain the others, and each was recorded to view afterwards, which caused a great deal of laughter and lots of surprises. The party began to break up around midnight, and all my customers went off to bed.

The manager asked me to join him at the bar for a nightcap, because he had to be on duty until the Americans retired. Suddenly, Madam poked her head round the door and said, in a loud voice, "I ain't got a guzzunder (chamber pot) in my room!" Then she shut the door behind her. The manager looked at me, speechless, but quickly rose to the occasion. He turned to me and said, "I can't leave the bar yet, so would you mind going to the maid's pantry on the first floor, where you will find the said article, and deliver it to room 5 – I think it is room 5." I went to the pantry as bidden, found a pot and walked to room 5 clutching the said object behind me. It was the wrong room.

Just then, I heard the Americans coming up the stairs. Not wanting to be seen clutching such an objet d'art, I placed it quickly on the landing and went to hide in the pantry, peeping through a gap in the door. As the Americans passed by, one was heard to say, "I guess this must be part of one of those quaint English customs." (Never mind that we were in Scotland.) At last, the coast was clear, so I dashed downstairs to find the right room number, climbed up again, retrieved the pot and tapped on Madam's door. I presented the pot to her handle first.

"You got one then," she said in a loud voice.

"Yes," I replied, "but I'm afraid it's a bit dusty."

"Never mind," she said, "I'll soon wash the b****** out!"

Later on, when we were staying overnight somewhere in Yorkshire, I was pleased to note that Betty and Jack were sitting together in the lounge. I was talking to the manageress when Jack approached, and I could see that he was very angry. Apparently, as he and Betty were sitting talking on the settee, Madam walked in and plonked herself between them. Jack got up and stormed into the garden. I explained to the manageress later on, but before then, I had a spot of quick thinking to rescue Betty. I went up to her and said, "Excuse me, but you are wanted on the telephone, and if you follow me I will show you where you can take the call." So, a very puzzled Betty followed me into the hall, and as soon as we were out of earshot, I turned and said, "He's in the garden."

Some seven years later, I took a tour around Devon and Cornwall. I was sitting at my usual corner table in one hotel, when a gentleman, who had been sitting across the other side of the room, came over to speak to me. "Do you remember me?" It was

Jack. "Come and meet my wife." You've guessed, of course, it was Betty. So my Cupid's bow did shoot straight after all.

Talking of shooting reminds me of another incident. On my way to a second night stop in Scotland, I was suddenly shot through the windscreen! I stood on the brake and could see the hole where the missile had come through the glass. I felt my chest, expecting to see a bloody hand, but there was none. Perhaps the blood hadn't seeped through my jacket yet. I looked down to the place where I had been shot, but nothing. It was then I realised that a passing car had thrown up a stone, which had come shooting through the windscreen into my chest. The passengers were very concerned but soon relaxed when I told them what was amiss; in fact, we had a good laugh about it later. However, it was no fun driving with a hole in the windscreen, and we had to delay our departure the next day to wait for a new screen to be fitted. I kept the stone as a souvenir.

Once, on the way to Scotland, we stayed for a night in a lakeside hotel in Cumbria. This time my wife and youngest daughter were on the tour with me. I had my usual room, and my wife and daughter shared a twin room which happened to have three beds in it. They retired at about eleven o'clock but were woken at about midnight by a gentle knock on the door. It was the young night manager, looking very embarrassed. He asked very politely if he could please remove the spare bed from their room, as they had a late-night guest and needed it for him. They readily agreed, and the young chap, with help from the night porter, tried to move the bed from the room.

They tried manhandling the bed through the door, knocking over a table lamp on the way, then they dropped it on the manager's foot, swung it round and swiped a picture from the wall. The porter leaned against the bathroom door, which swung open, catapulting him into the shower cubicle. They manoeuvred it through the bedroom door, crushing a potted palm in the corridor, then they scraped a slice out of the ferule on the banister, tripped over a spare blanket and very nearly sent the whole lot crashing down the stairs.

My wife and daughter were in silent hysterics by now, trying not to laugh out loud, and they couldn't get back to sleep for giggling.

Drivers on these long tours usually had a table to themselves, often in the corner of the dining room so that they could keep an eye on the guests to make sure that all was well. By and large, the drivers got on well with the hotel staff throughout the British Isles, and there were only one or two exceptions, where management tried to put us in inferior accommodation. In one hotel, the driver's room had been converted hastily and still had the brass plate on the door which said "engaged" when the door was locked. A phone call to head office soon put this right.

Talking of corner tables reminds me of the time I went for lunch in a hotel in Edinburgh. I sat at my usual table, alone, by the partition, where the waiting staff came and went from the kitchen. The head waitress had a sense of humour like mine, and we often shared a joke. My soup was placed in front of me, and I had just picked up my spoon, when I felt a movement on my left shoulder. Out of the corner of my eye, I saw a huge spider making its way towards my neck. Being terrified of spiders, I leapt up with a shout, scattering the table, soup, roll and cutlery all over the floor. The whole staff were doubled up with laughter at my expense – it was a toy spider which moved when the rubber bulb at the end of an attached tube was squeezed. Was my face red! I took it in good part but was determined to exact my revenge one day. A couple of years later, I was in Scotland on a family holiday in the car and had stopped for a break in Edinburgh, when an idea came into my head. I called at the hotel and, walking into the dining room, saw the same head waitress and asked if lunch was ready for my party of forty. The look of blind panic on her face was a joy to behold. There was frantic scrabbling around until someone had the presence of mind to check the bookings. The joke was on them. We all had a good laugh and then we settled down for a very pleasant lunch with my family. No spiders this time!

On one coach tour, we were in a very remote area of the Scottish Highlands, when one of my lady passengers, Mrs Rose, was taken very ill, with a suspected heart attack. The hotel manager immediately summoned the local doctor, who said that the lady needed to be in hospital urgently. Unfortunately, the helicopter was not available, and the local ambulance was on another emergency call. The manager said he would drive the lady, but she really needed to lie down, so I offered my coach. The manager rushed to his office to retrieve an old stretcher from the storeroom, and a couple of blankets, and following the doctor's instructions, we managed to get the lady on to the stretcher. After a very brief discussion, it was decided to gain entry to the coach via the rear emergency exit, where there were no stairs to negotiate. However, this meant lifting the stretcher up high enough to slide it onto the floor between the rear seat and the one in front. We enlisted the help of a couple of men from the kitchen and, with excellent teamwork, soon had Mrs Rose safely installed in the coach. The doctor travelled with Mrs Rose, and her husband in the coach, and the manager followed behind in his car with the two members of staff, in case they were needed. Before we left, the doctor spoke to the medics at the hospital so that they were prepared, and off we went.

Mrs Rose looked in a bad way, so I set off at a fair speed, but at the same time, tried to make the journey as smooth as possible. However, the journey was not without incident. A local police car was on patrol and, seeing my coach moving fairly fast, decided to investigate and flagged me down. I think they suspected that I was drunk. I quickly started to explain the situation, but the doctor, whom the policemen knew, took over and said how urgent it was that the lady had treatment. Without delay, the policemen said they would escort us. So, with blues and twos blaring out, we made short work of the rest of the journey. The hospital medical staff were waiting for us and rushed Mrs Rose into the cardiac unit, where she received the expert care which saved her life.

Mr and Mrs Rose had to miss the rest of their holiday, but that was a small price to pay for being alive. The hotel manager gave me a lift to the hospital the next evening, and we were so pleased to see Mrs Rose sitting in the chair next to her bed, looking so much better. The hotel manager said the couple could stay at the hotel free of charge for as long as they needed to, until Mrs Rose was well enough to go home. True Scottish hospitality. They took up his kind offer for a few days once the hospital allowed Mrs Rose to leave, then their holiday insurance paid for them to have a private hire car to take them home. I think that was a holiday they would never forget.

On my part, I was so relieved that Mrs Rose made a good recovery, and I would like to thank her for the lovely letter she sent me, thanking me for my help. I was only too glad to have been of some use.

I was very fortunate on my tours that I rarely had anyone ill, just an occasional hangover, and a good breakfast often put that right.

On one Scottish trip we stayed in a remote hotel in the Highlands. It was quite a sprawling building, having had numerous extensions built over the years. There were lots of nooks and crannies, staircases, short corridors and different levels. Quite a labyrinth. It was decorated with stuffed deer heads, ancient weapons, tartan curtains and carpets, and dark wood panelling here and there. Every decorating cliché you could imagine, which made it very atmospheric. The hotel was set in beautiful surroundings, with views to die for, and it was so quiet, all you could hear was the distant bleating from the local sheep and the sound of running water in the stream which flowed nearby on its way to the small lake (or should that be loch?).

My wife, Alice, and daughter Susan came on this trip. They had no special treatment, except we shared a dining table instead of my usual single, and they understood that I was on duty twenty-four seven (we didn't share a table at any other hotels we stayed in). Alice and Susan shared a twin room on the ground floor, which is the room I normally had, and I was put in a small, single room on the second floor. We had a hearty dinner, then quite a number of the guests congregated in the bar for a nightcap. The bar was the cosiest room in the hotel, with its blazing fire and friendly barman. People were relaxed and enjoying themselves, playing cards, dominoes or darts, or just chatting. I allowed myself one whisky, just to be sociable, then decided to retire, with the excuse that I had paperwork to do. It is not a good idea for a coach driver to be tired or hungover the next day, so I said goodnight to Alice and Susan, who were also ready to retire. I wondered whether to warn them about "Green Jean" but did not want to scare them or put ideas in their heads. So, it was, "Goodnight, sleep well." This is Susan's account the next morning, of what happened.

"We said goodnight to Dad and made our way to our room, number 12. Mum and I both felt uneasy because there was a strange atmosphere in that room. It is a good job it was not 13, because Mum was very superstitious and would never ever stay in number 13. Anyway, we were both feeling a bit spooked, so I checked inside the huge oak wardrobe and Mum checked under the beds. Everything was normal. We locked the bedroom door and closed the window. We did our ablutions, climbed into our beds and snuggled under the blankets because the evening had turned quite chilly. I don't know how long I had been in bed, but I had just about dozed off when I felt something icy cold brush against my cheek. I thought perhaps it was Mum, so I opened my eyes to see what she wanted, but she was still in her bed. I became aware of something in the corner of my eye, so I turned my head – at the end of my bed there was a green, luminous outline of a person!

"I felt like screaming but instead pulled the covers over my head and tried to think what to do. Then I heard Mum moving about in her bed and rocking it, making a bit of a noise. I thought about asking her if she was OK but didn't want to startle her. Eventually, once my heartbeat had calmed down, I fell asleep but woke early the next morning. Mum was already up and about. She asked if I'd slept alright, and I told her what I had seen. She then told me that she didn't shake her bed, but it had been rocked by something, and also she had seen a green glow at the end of her bed. She also added that if I had spoken to her she would have screamed, because she was so scared. We wondered if someone was playing tricks on us, so we had a really good look around the room for anything suspicious – we found nothing. No secret wires, lights or switches, etc. – nothing.

"When we saw Dad at breakfast, he asked if we'd slept well. We told him what had happened and he said he had wondered whether to tell us about 'Green Jean' or not. Green Jean had been a serving girl in the big house (now part of the hotel), when she came to an untimely death (he didn't know the details). It seems that her spirit still visits from time to time, so Dad had seen her on numerous occasions either in room 12 or 13.

"However, that was not the end of strange happenings. At breakfast, we discovered that the couple in room 13 had woken in the night to the sound of running water. The man got out of bed to investigate to find the bath full to overflowing, which was rather odd when neither of them had used the bath, only the shower. Evidently, Green Jean sometimes moved things about. On a previous visit, a guest complained at the reception desk that the cleaner had moved her toothbrush from the basin to the old fireplace in her room (12) and had squeezed toothpaste out all over her box of pills. Another time, a guest found several fir cones under her pillow, and another person found their shoes full of water in the morning. These are all events recounted by Dad *after* we had stayed the night in the haunted room!

"I must say, Mum and I were quite happy to leave."

On the same tour, we had to take a ferry, so before I dropped off the passengers, I had to turn the coach around on the dock. This is when the fun started. I enlisted the help of people sitting at the back and asked them to keep an eye on the edge, unless they wanted to swim. Now, what most people don't realise is that there is a large overhang between the rear wheels and the end of the vehicle, so all was ready. I knew that there was loads of room to manoeuvre, and so I began reversing slowly. As the coach approached the edge of the dock, there were loud shouts from the back urging me to stop, but I continued, knowing exactly how much room I had. When I came to a stop, with the rear end hanging over the dock, I let the passengers off and, luckily, when they had a look, they realised I had tricked them, and most saw the funny side. I had one or two silly tricks up my sleeve.

When we came to a steep hill, I would ask the passengers to lean forward, because the weight distribution would help us up the incline. Most people joined in, either because it was a bit of fun or they genuinely believed me. Likewise, if we were going under a low bridge, I would get them to duck down so that the downward pressure would make the coach a few vital inches lower. There was always someone who made my day.

Another trick was when the passengers were seated back on the coach after a stop. I always did a head count, then I would say, "Put your hand up if you are not here." I caught someone out every time. Some people are so gullible or perhaps they just don't listen. I find that if you speak with authority, with a serious face, and particularly if you are wearing a uniform, some people will believe anything!

Chapter Fifteen
Shetland Bus

One day, my gaffer sent for me and told me that the boss at head office wanted to see me. What had I done wrong now?

Arriving at head office, very smartly dressed in uniform, I was ushered into the inner sanctum with another coach courier called Arthur. We were told that we had been chosen to drive for a new tour to Shetland and were given a folder full of details to study. Mine was to be the very first ever organised tour of Shetland if I chose to accept. When I arrived home, I discussed the tour with Alice, and we both agreed that I should go ahead.

I had barely heard of the mysterious, remote Shetland Islands but knew they were somewhere far north, off the coast of Scotland but probably nearer to Norway. So a new adventure was about to begin. It was arranged that we should spend two nights on our way to Aberdeen, where we would board the ferry MV *St Clair*, a neat 3,300-ton vessel, which had previously been built and owned by a Norwegian company. This boat/ship would take us to Shetland. When does a boat become a ship?

Apparently, a ship can carry a boat, but not the other way around.

After a few trips across the sea to Lerwick, I became well known to the crew, and a grand lot of people they were too, always ready to help, especially in rough weather. The chief steward was amazing. He could serve eleven breakfasts in one go. Full cooked breakfasts,

Percy's Bus

with the boat pitching about on the ocean, which was often quite lively. He could balance all of the plates on his hands and arms, without any plate touching the plate below, and without dropping anything, in spite of the rolling deck. Try it sometime – four or five plates in one hand, two on each arm and two in the spare hand. No, he wasn't an octopus!

It was on one of these trips that I had a problem with one passenger. He was a retired miner who had booked with my company, for a fourteen-day trip to Shetland. He arrived at our departure point wearing a battered cloth cap, a shabby old suit carrying a very small suitcase, which probably contained a shirt, razor, soap, a pair of underpants and pyjamas, and very little else. He was a decent bloke but had a very strong, overwhelming aroma about him. There was no single accommodation on this trip, and no-one seemed very keen to share with the miner, so I was the obvious choice. On the way to Aberdeen, I managed to secure single accommodation for him in the hotels, but this was not the end of things. The first night in the hotel, the miner was refused entry into the restaurant because he refused to remove his cap. I had to do something, so I arranged for his meal to be served on a tray, which he ate in a corner of the lounge. I felt sorry for the old boy (whom I shall call Old Bill) because he had paid like everyone else on the tour, so why not be treated like everyone else? My next problem was on board ship. I told the Purser about Old Bill, and he promised to do what he could. The ship sailed from Aberdeen to Lerwick, 128 miles, which was an eleven-hour journey, three times a week, so it was always busy, and on this occasion, full. It was primarily a cargo ship, and the islands received most of their goods by sea, their main export by sea being sheep and a few pigs, so cabin space was limited. We sailed from Aberdeen at 17:00 hours on a calm sea, for once. It can get very rough crossing the Pentland Firth, but thankfully I am a good sailor – it must be my Norfolk heritage. Before we set sail, I watched as a beautiful Bentley car was hoisted on to the forward deck, where it was lashed down for safety. Having settled my passengers into their cabins, I had a call over the intercom to report to the purser, who was in charge of cabin allocations. He told me to remove my luggage from the cabin I had been assigned (sharing with Old Bill) and take it to the one which had just been cancelled by a local, who had been taken ill in Aberdeen, so his four-berth cabin was ready for my use. I presumed that would mean Old Bill would have a cabin to himself... but no!

Just before the ship was due to sail, a young RAF officer came on board and *demanded*, rather discourteously, that the purser find him a berth. One obviously does *not* demand anything from a senior merchant navy officer with a chest covered in medal ribbons. So the purser, very politely offered him the top bunk in Old Bill's cabin. The young man picked up his bag, without a word of thanks, and went in search of his cabin. He opened the door without knocking and flung his bag onto the top bunk.

"What are you doing here? This bunk is for my driver," yelled Old Bill.

RAF stormed back to the purser, who was waiting for him. "There is a scruffy old chap in that cabin, telling me he is sharing with his driver," he shouted.

The purser replied in a very dignified manner, "The gentleman in question was indeed sharing with his driver, who has agreed to sleep in the lounge so that you may have a bunk for the night. If you look out of the porthole, you will see his Bentley parked on the forward deck. The old gentleman is a somewhat eccentric millionaire."

The RAF chap retreated quite red-faced – I hope he learned that good manners count, no matter what the circumstances. I saluted the purser; how he kept a straight face I shall never know.

On these trips to Shetland, I could not take my coach, as it was much too big to be transported and too big for the local roads, so I had a chance to take in the scenery whilst local drivers took over with much "cosier" buses. After breakfast on the ship, we were transported to the other side of the main island, to Scalloway, where we stayed in a small hotel which was only just big enough to cater for us. It was a pleasant family-run hotel on the seafront with views of the islands of Trondra, East and West Burra, and many more small islands inhabited by sheep, which were ferried in rowing boats across the sea to graze on the fresh green grass. The hotel owners were unaccustomed to having so many guests at one time, and this led to several minor inconveniences, such as nowhere to hang clothes in the bedrooms, lack of soap and towels, but these problems were soon sorted. Hospitality was second to none.

It was so peaceful there, practically no traffic, only the occasional sheep wandering along the road. Our week's stay was fully occupied by many coach trips. The local driver complained about the increase in traffic, and on one full day trip, I counted seven cars on the road, and that was heavy traffic! We used to go to the Esha Ness Lighthouse, which was really remote. To get to it, we had to pass through a farmyard and make sure the gate was closed after us so that the sheep could not escape. The lighthouse keeper lived in a cottage next to the light, with his sister, who was an expert knitter of anything in the local traditional patterns of "Fair Isle". She could turn her hands to hats, scarves, gloves shawls, etc. made with the lovely soft Shetland wool. When we visited, she ended up with a huge order book, which she shared out amongst friends and neighbours to satisfy demand. When leaving the lighthouse on one occasion, it was my job to open the gate for the bus to pass through and then close it behind by giving the self-closing gate a push to set it on its way to the self-locking device. I was in a hurry to get out of the very cold wind which had suddenly arisen ("hurry" is not a word used in Shetland), so I didn't notice a car coming along the lane. I hopped onto our bus, and the driver said, "Do you realise you have just shut the gate on our local MP – Joe Grimond?" I got the driver to stop so that I could go and apologise to the MP. He was very gracious and had a good laugh about it.

On the way back to the hotel we noticed a sheep with its head stuck in a rusty tin can. The driver pulled up, we explained the situation, briefly, to the passengers, then spent a good ten minutes trying to rescue the silly beast. Somehow, the can became dislodged and the sheep seemed no worse for wear, so the driver picked up the can as a souvenir and we got back on the bus to a huge cheer, and lots of jokes and puns about shepherds and sheep.

Q. What do you call a sheep with a tin can on its head?
A. Call it anything you like – it can't hear you because it has a tin can on its head.

Another interesting trip was a whole-day excursion to the most northerly point of the British Isles – Muckle Flugga. (What a great name!) There was an RAF station there, which was classed as an overseas base and was mainly a weather station, manned by a handful of men. In those days, the base was only accessible by a narrow road or by helicopter. The latter could not be used in very windy conditions, which were a frequent occurrence. A wind speed of over 125 miles per hour had been recorded at the lighthouse there. One windy day, a large piece of equipment was blown from its housing and embedded itself in a huge fifty-ton block of concrete. Such was the force of the wind. Shetlanders never underestimate the weather! They have a saying: "We have six months' winter and six months' bad weather." There were no standard trees on the Shetland Isles, only the odd dwarf tree growing in a sheltered spot, because of the strong winds. Luckily for me, the weather was not bad most of the time whilst I was there.

A local retired merchant seaman called Han, with whom I had chatted quite often in the hotel bar, asked me if I would like to see a giant skua. I had heard about these birds, with a wingspan of around five feet, so agreed to go with him. We set off uphill and he handed me a sizeable stick with the words, "You'll be needing this, laddie." I questioned him, but he just smiled and said, "Copy me." We reached the footpath which traversed the cliff top, and I held my stick above my head, just like Han. After a few seconds, a huge bird rose up into the air and started to divebomb us – the stick was for our protection, because one hit from that sharp beak would inflict a lot of damage to one's person. This bird was soon joined by others, and we were kept busy waving our sticks around, fending off the attacks. I felt very vulnerable, because I could feel a tremendous rush of air as they attacked. I did not fancy being skewered by a giant skua! Han thought we'd had enough, and besides, it was time for his wee dram in the well-stocked hotel bar. This had over thirty brands of whisky, many of which were single malt. I have a liking for the occasional drop of quality malt and had a different one each evening before going to bed. It was a luxury for me, because I wasn't driving. If I was driving the next day, then I would dilute the whisky with water.

Touring around the Shetlands was very pleasant, with magnificent scenery and tranquillity, but involved lots of transferring to small buses and taking ferries from island to island with unusual names, such as Yell, Unst, Fetlar, Foula, Fair Isle and Whalsay, with equally strange settlement names which had a Norse influence; after all, we were not far from Norway, and there are remains of Norse settlements on Shetland.

The Scottish accent here also has a touch of Scandinavian, as do local people's names. Settlements such as Fladderbister, Uyeasound, Easter Skeld, Ollaberry and Haroldswick were examples of outside influences. The latter place had a post office which was famous for selling the highest number of winning Premium Bonds per head of population in Scotland. Haroldswick also had another claim to fame, and that is an unusual quarry nearby. They excavated here for a very soft stone (mineral) which could be ground into talcum powder; right next to this, they mined a very hard stone which was used for lining furnaces.

On our way round Shetland, passing the northern tip of Basta Voe, there is a narrow strip of land which separates St Magnus Bay on the left (Atlantic Ocean) and Sullom Voe on the right (North Sea). It is possible, from the top of the mound, to throw a stone into the Atlantic Ocean and, without moving, throw a stone into the North Sea. The coach parties took to this experiment with great enthusiasm, and there were stones flying about all over the place. I lobbed quite a few stones myself – it was fun.

Our coach driver, called Hind, had a car hire business-come-taxi firm. He showed us his three vehicles, which were immaculate but were not in huge demand. The most interesting one was an old T model Ford, which was a "convertible", but not in the way you might imagine. This vehicle had a detachable body and, with the addition of different bodies, could be used as a lorry or bus, or even a hearse.

Some evenings, if I had completed my duties, I used to enjoy strolling along the sea front to investigate the numerous sheds there. One was a lifeboat station. They made me most welcome when I popped my head round the door and offered to take me on a sea trial with them when they completed the boat overhaul. Unfortunately, I was never there at the right time, but I salute the brave people who voluntarily man these stations, especially in the treacherous waters around Shetland.

Another shed was where the day's catch of lobsters was kept in large tanks of seawater. Each lobster had a big rubber band wrapped around their huge claw, for safety reasons – so that they did not attack each other, and also so they did not nip the fishermen. I declined the offer of holding one – those claws looked rather lethal!

Anywhere you went on Shetland, you were always greeted very warmly and offered hospitality, tea, whisky, scones and pancakes. The "wee dram" of whisky was usually about four fingers, neat. On occasion, a little water could be added, but *never* anything else. Why murder a beautiful, smooth malt?

Mr H Smith was another local character. He owned an old fishing boat which he used to take groups from Scalloway to the island of Foula to see the local wildlife. This was only a fair-weather trip but proved most enjoyable. Some of the passengers were allowed to take the helm, under supervision, whilst Mr Smith pointed out the wildlife – a small group of seals and thousands of sea birds. Late spring was a good time to go, because the island would be bordered with sea pinks in full bloom, looking like an iced cake.

How I Became the Earl of Scalloway

On the return from Shetland, we used to stay overnight at a hotel in the north of England. After unloading the luggage I went to park the coach in the allotted spot, then went into the hotel to sign the party in. When I looked at the register, I noted two signatures of very important people just above the space for mine. The manager saw me looking and, knowing me quite well, said, "Keep up the good appearance." So I signed "The Earl of Scalloway and party". The manager replied, "That will do nicely, My Lord, thank you." Just then, a gentleman had approached the desk to ask if he could have a room for him and his wife for the night. As he signed the register, he commented on the distinguished guests signed into the register. With a nod and wink, the manager turned to me and said, "Is everything all right, My Lord?"

I replied, "Indeed it is." With that response I turned and went to my room to change for dinner. I was sitting at my single table in the dining room when the couple who registered after me came in, and I noticed that they had a good look in my direction.

The next morning, I was unlocking my coach when the same couple came outside to go to their car. What amazed expressions they had on their faces. I think in the next few weeks they must have dined out on the tale of the "Earl of Scalloway" driving a coach.

PS. If there is a real Earl of Scalloway, then I apologise for using his title, but it was done in the best possible taste! Thank you.

Chapter Sixteen
My Father and Grandfathers

My paternal grandparents, James and Clara Taylor

My parents, Ernest and Eliza Taylor, on VE Day

The following short chapter is taken from notes left by my father, who had begun to write his life story. These are his own words:

> It is possible to go back in memory eighty-odd years, and I am trying to piece together my boyhood years from 1887 up to about 1913. That period embraces the end of Victoria's reign, the whole of Edward VII and into the reign of George V. Quite a lot of that time was spent with my uncle and aunt in London, where I was born (Queen's Park) on 1st June 1884. My first recollection was of Queen Victoria's Golden Jubilee in 1887. I was three years old, and I can, in my imagination, feel my father's arms around me as he carried me to see the decorations and pretty lights in the City. At that time, my father was employed by a firm of solicitors on Threadneedle Street. He was a law writer (pre-stenograph machine) and attended court to record all that was said during trials, by hand. He was an accomplished shorthand writer, using his own system,

and was completely ambidextrous so that when one hand became tired, he could write just as well with the other. His claim to fame was that he wrote down the whole of the Titchborne trial, which then was the longest trial ever recorded, with over a million words.

My father's health broke down and he was advised by his doctor to leave London, which was not a very healthy place to live, so we moved to Norfolk, the county of his birth and where we had family roots. He opened a fancy goods shop in East Dereham, a pleasant small market town. When I was old enough, I went to a little private school, for a couple of years, to learn my pothooks (letters), alphabet and numbers. After bouts of usual children's ailments, mumps, measles, etc., I was taken to my uncle's house in London, to recuperate, which seems very strange with hindsight, especially since my father had left London for his health's sake.

My uncle had a son, my cousin, almost the same age as me, so we were good companions for each other. We attended school together, which was another private one, in a room at the Army and Navy store, near Embankment. The governor's daughter ran a little kindergarten for children of the staff. My uncle, a director of a coal firm, lived nearby in St George's Square, and during holidays, my cousin and I spent a lot of time by the river, where there was always so much to see. We had access to numerous river craft, with journeys on tugboats and lots of visits to Battersea Park and Kew Gardens.

Occasionally, we were guests of tugboat captains who collected full barges from Tilbury and other docks. London was then a bustling city with ships arriving from all over the world. The roads were busy too, not with motorised vehicles but horse-drawn ones, because there were no motors on the roads at that time.

Some Saturdays my cousin and I had two pennyworth of bus rides (horse-drawn, of course) through the City.

Sometimes we walked to Victoria Station and took a bus to Liverpool Street Station. We always tried sit as close to the drivers as possible so that we could listen to their stories, which were most illuminating, being very ungrammatical and full of Cockney humour and rhyming slang. Sometimes a journey would be held up by a military parade, especially in Whitehall and Buckingham Palace Road, being just before the Boer War. It all added to the excitement.

During the summer holidays we sometimes visited relatives in Norfolk. The Bush family was a favourite because of our huge cousins. They were both a piece over six foot six inches tall – real giants! One cousin was a policeman in London and the other was a farmer in Norfolk. The farming cousin was incredibly strong and would hold out his arm horizontally so that my cousin and I could swing from it. I remember his arm, solid with muscle, which made gripping quite difficult. Their mother, my aunt, was a tiny woman, and I often wonder how she came to bear such large sons. When aunt wanted the donkey cart, my cousin would jump over the field gate, pick up the donkey and carry it to the waiting cart. A bail of straw was tossed as easily as a pancake, and he would delight in throwing us boys into the air with squeals of delight and catching us in his great arms.

After about two years in London, I returned home and entered a church school, where I stayed for about five years, then finished off at a grammar school. The church school was a strict Anglican one, and we had to go to church three times a week, and every day during Lent. The church had old box pews which were exceedingly uncomfortable. There was a beadle with a long stick, which he used to crack over one's head if he thought you were misbehaving. We found that the panelling under the seats of the pews would slide, so during the Litany, when every word was spoken, with one eye on the beadle, we would

My Father and Grandfathers

wriggle through from one pew to another and sometimes even play marbles. Confession is good for the soul, eh?

I am not going to write a full history of my life but an abridged one. Next in importance was my apprenticeship to the watch, jewellery and allied trades. During my training, with the Worshipful Company of Goldsmiths, I was invited to visit the vault at the Bank of England. What an experience – millions of pounds' worth of gold bullion. I was even allowed to hold one of the very heavy bars. Once my training was complete, it was time to earn a living. When the day came, my father gave me five sovereigns and said, "Don't look home for help – stand on your own feet and make me proud." So I was on my own. I had several jobs including one in Newark, where I met my future wife, Eliza, but the most important job I had was when I moved to Lincoln to work for Mr James Ward Usher.

It was in 1911, aged twenty-eight, that I applied for a post as assistant in a high-class jewellery and fine art shop in Lincoln, owned by Mr Usher. An advert in the *London Chronicle* read "Wanted. Experienced Assistant". Not being very comfortable in my present employment, I applied, without response. I thought nothing of this because other applications had received no response. This was in May. However, in August, I received a telegram: "Come and see me. Usher." I paid no attention at the time, but about two weeks later, I received another telegram: "Imperative you see me today. Usher. Lincoln." This gave me the impression that I should attend. I duly travelled to Lincoln, having made an appointment, but on reaching the shop at around 3pm I was told that Mr Usher was not available until after his principal meal of the day, which was about 4.30 to 5.00pm. I was advised to have a walk around the city and return at 6.30pm.

Mr Usher styled himself as a two-meal-a-day man and said that no-one required more than two meals a day, and judging by his actions and behaviour, it might be so. He generally rose about 9.00am, and after a very substantial breakfast of two or three courses, lasting up to about 11.00am, he would then be ready to attend to the mail, followed by what he called his constitutional walk, returning about 3.30pm, and then he would prepare for his main meal. I have known him to eat one whole roast duck with all the trimmings, followed by a pudding, washed down with a fine port, accompanied with fruit, chocolates and tea. He really did have a voracious appetite and would consume a whole chicken or a whole plate full of lamb cutlets. He also had a pension for drinking sour milk, so it was hardly surprising that about once a month he had a bilious attack and I would be despatched to the chemist for his Special Black Draught.

But I digress; I returned for my interview at six thirty. No mention was made of the job, but Mr Usher went straight into talking about his collection. He was a proud showman, and very soon I was fascinated by his collection and experiences. Time slipped by and I found that I had missed the last train home, and no mention of the situation had been made, neither had he offered me any refreshment, although his housekeeper (he was a bachelor) had brought him his nightcap of warm milk and biscuits. It was then very late, so I suggested that perhaps he could offer me hospitality for the night. Oh, no! I had to go to an hotel. It was then after 11.00pm, and so over to the old Spread Eagle. It was closed and in darkness, but I managed to get hold of the boot boy and, after much persuasion, was given a bed for the night.

I had another appointment with Mr Usher at 11.30 the next morning; it was then I made my demands. Did he want to employ me, and what would be the pay? After much discussion and argument, we came to an agreement, and I was duly installed as first assistant.

I moved my family to a terraced house in Lincoln, and thus began my life in the employment of an extraordinary man. One of my early duties was clock winding. This entailed visiting the big houses in Lincoln and winding, regulating and maintaining their valuable clocks. I was also responsible for installing and maintaining the large blue and gold clock which hangs in one of the entrance lobbies at the west end of Lincoln Cathedral.

But a little more about my employer.

James Ward Usher was the oldest son of James Usher of Lincoln, who founded a jewellery shop in 1837, in Lincoln. James Ward was born on 1st January 1845. He went into his father's business, hence the name Usher and Son. James Ward became Sheriff of Lincoln in 1916, having made a name for himself as a collector of fine art and a businessman.

In 1883, James Ward Usher had visited an auction house for the first time, and the sight of so many beautiful items set him off on the road to collecting. As well as attending sale rooms, he travelled thousands of miles visiting galleries and private houses to see as much as possible and to increase his knowledge. Gradually, his collection became his ruling passion, and he came to rely on me more and more in the shop so that he could enjoy his hobby. As I said, he was an extraordinary man. He could be conceited but was fiercely loyal. He had an amazing memory and could recite huge chunks of Milton or Shakespeare, just to impress people. He was also a fine artist, and he painted meticulous watercolour pictures of many of the items in his collection, especially the watches, which were collated into a beautiful book, which is housed in the gallery. This book took ten years to complete and was privately published, with only 184 copies being sold. He had many offers for the copyright of the book, but he refused to sell. He thought if the book became too well known, it might encourage burglars, which was an obsession of his. When he was engaged in drawing and painting his beloved treasures, we all had very strict instructions not to disturb him. On one occasion, I remember him saying, "I will not see anyone – not even royalty!" One day, Lord Roseberry came to see the renowned collection, but Mr Usher would not leave his drawing to entertain his Lordship.

One could say that he was very eccentric, but he was a very astute businessman who held stock in more than fifty companies. His life was his collection, and on many occasions he would invite a chance acquaintance to view the collection, if they showed an interest, even being given the privilege of handling the priceless treasures. I would often be summoned to help lay out some of the finer specimens. There was a Faberge watch, and a watch that had belonged to Mary, Queen of Scots, plus a ring watch made for George III.

James Ward Usher decided to market the Lincoln Imp. He gained the monopoly on this for six years, and it proved to be a tremendous success, which accounted for much of the business, as orders flooded in from all over the world. The imp had a legend attached to it: "One day, the Devil decided to send his imps to cause havoc on earth. One imp rode on the north wind to Lincoln, where he bade the wind wait for him whilst he went inside. He tore prayer books, broke candles, scattered vestments around, until an angel in the angel choir came down and turned him into stone as a punishment. His little figure can be seen today between two arches near the High Altar. As for the north wind, it is said to be waiting at the north corner of the Cathedral, even today."

A variety of imps were made in gold and silver as pendants, charms, tie pins, cufflinks, etc., and were sold worldwide. We often had orders addressed just to the Lincoln Imp Shop, Lincoln, it was so well known. An American came into the shop one day and said he wanted to buy the shop, its contents and Mr Usher's collection. He laid his cheque book on the table and said, "Name your price."

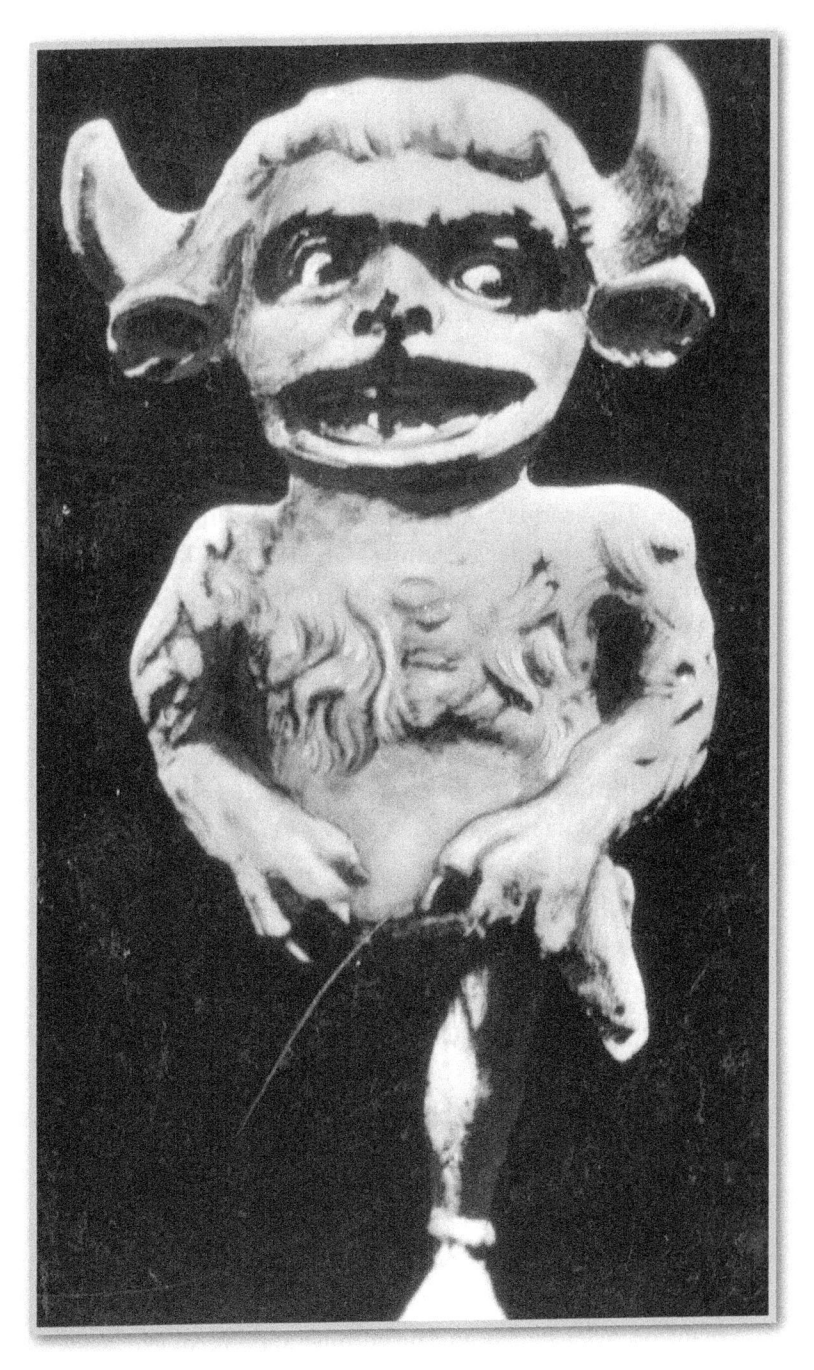

The Lincoln Imp

Mr Usher refused, stating, "I am a bachelor, and these treasures are my family and my life – I will never sell."

JWU was very proud of his good name. Somewhat conceited and selfish in small ways, rather than mean. He never carried money, except when travelling out of Lincoln, and then he would account for every penny spent. He usually borrowed my copy of the *Echo* to read, which only cost a halfpenny. He often travelled on the trams and would come into the shop and tell one of the staff to go and pay such and such conductor, who had trusted him. He never owed money to anyone.

His only near relative was a younger brother who was a farmer. The brother got into financial difficulties, and one morning, a horse dealer came to see JWU and threatened to make his brother bankrupt. Mr Usher flared up in anger. "How dare you threaten my family! How much does he owe?"

Mr Usher wrote out a cheque for £200 and said, "Don't you ever threaten my family again." This, however, opened the floodgates for all the other creditors. The final settlement came to over £2,000.

When JWU made his weekly trips to London, he tended to leave arrangements to the last minute. I think he relied on his good name to get him by. Frequently, one of us would run to the station to ask the guard to hold the train for Mr Usher, and they would usually comply. Sometimes we would move the regulator clock forward, so that he would be on time.

When I first started working in the shop, which was a very high-class business, I had to deal with the local gentry, wealthy businesspeople and numerous visitors from abroad. One particular client was a Mr S, who was, unbeknown to me, a millionaire who had a very large mansion, well-staffed and beautifully appointed, as I was to discover later. My first encounter with him was over some Lincoln Imp brooches, which he had asked to see, so I brought out the ordinary tray. He said, "They are not what I want. I usually have the diamond set ones." So I duly fetched the roll of eight diamond imps from the safe to show him. "Ah, yes," he said, and proceeded to roll them up to put in his pocket. I became somewhat alarmed.

"Excuse me," I said, "but who are you?"

"I'm so sorry," replied Mr S, "you are new here. Please have each one put in a case and send them to me. I'm a friend of Mr Usher."

I verified this before sending them, and Mr Usher told me who he was, and that I was to let him have anything he took a fancy to. Mr S was a widower, and any lady who was a guest in his house would be given a diamond-studded imp. If the lady was dining, the first course would be a covered plate, and under the cover would be an item of jewellery. I also had the job of going to his house each week to wind and maintain the clocks and on these visits was expected to take a box of collectables for Mr S to look at and perhaps buy.

One Saturday morning, after the '14–'18 war, I had returned to my old job, when I had a recurrence of malaria, which caused ague and much trembling. Mr S noticed my shaking hand as I tried to wind the clock. "And what party have you been to?" he enquired. I told him it was not drink but malaria. He immediately summoned the butler and got him to bring up a bottle of fine '64 brandy. I was handed a good glassful and told to drink it slowly. I must have passed out, because I woke up four hours later with a splitting headache but no shaking. The butler handed me the bottle, with the instructions from Mr S to take it with me and use it for when I had another attack. This was only one of the many generosities given to me.

Now, James Ward Usher had no children to leave his fortune to and often spoke about bequeathing his beloved collection to the City of Lincoln, the city of his birth, but

The Usher Gallery, Lincoln

he had not made a will. He became ill whilst holidaying in Wales and so cut his trip short. He took to his bed and the doctor was summoned. The doctor said that his condition was very serious and JWU would not last for more than a few days. I persuaded him to call in a solicitor so that he could make a will, otherwise his fantastic collection would have to be broken up and sold on his death. A solicitor was summoned, and Mr Usher made his will so that the entire collection of paintings, fine art and watches went to the city he loved, and the remainder of his estate was sufficient to have a gallery built to house everything – The Usher Gallery.

It was whilst I was working for Mr Usher that the Great War began. There was no conscription to start with, so I continued in employment, but then occurred a great family tragedy. My poor father was killed in a Zeppelin raid on East Dereham in Norfolk on 8th September 1915. It was thought that the Zeppelins were heading for the port

My father, Ernest Taylor, in RFC uniform, 1915

of King's Lynn, but the weather changed, so they had to turn round, and instead of their intended target, they offloaded the bombs over East Dereham.

My father, James Taylor, had gone to post a letter when the Zeppelins had released their deadly load. He and five other people were killed. I immediately went and signed up for the Royal Flying Corps to get my revenge on the Hun! Mr Usher said he would keep my job for my return, and off I went. After a very basic training course, it was decided to send my unit to Egypt, where I served as a cook. I suppose the top brass considered me useless for heavy work, and my light touch for watch making could be transferred to the field kitchen. It was no joke cooking in that heat, with all the flies, but we all got on with the job. I contracted malaria at one point, and that would stay with me for the rest of my life, with occasional re-occurrences. After the war, I returned to my job with Mr Usher and managed the shop until my retirement.

I will tell you about the Romany gipsy woman who was a regular visitor to the shop. She used to collect unusual second-hand gold jewellery but always had a tale to tell about each piece. She could tell you where it was from and something about the previous owner. It was very uncanny. One particular day she came into the shop and asked to see the item I had in the back room. How did she know I had that morning taken in a stunning gold necklace set with lapis lazuli? She held it in her hands and proceeded to give me its history. It was from Egypt, and the first owner had been a high-ranking lady who had met a dark fate. In fact, she said that every owner had met with tragedy. It was true, anyone could see it was Egyptian, but how did she know that the owner had indeed met with a sad end? It was in our shop because a local member of the nobility had brought it in to sell. He had bought it for his daughter for her last birthday, but she had tragically been killed whilst out riding. The gipsy did not buy it, because, she said, "It has bad vibrations and is a bad-luck piece." She also said I should get rid of it as soon as possible and not let any female members of my family touch it. Amazingly, I sold it the same day to an American tourist, who thought it was great to have such a history – he obviously did not believe the story of tragedy.

When I was made manager, I was able to move my family to a large house on the edge of town, overlooking the West Common. It was from here that we could watch the horse racing which was held there before the track closed and the Lincolnshire Handicap moved to Doncaster. We would be fascinated to hear the jockeys shouting to each other to come through or hold back. Does that happen today?

This marks the end of my father's notes, so back to Percy.

My father was a true gentleman with impeccable manners but was quite strict with us boys, as he needed to be, because we were always up to some form of mischief (especially me).

Now some words about my maternal grandfather.

George Perfect, my grandfather, was a very imposing Victorian gentleman. He was a cabinet maker and builder and lived in Newark, Nottinghamshire. I was always a bit afraid of him with his dark eyes and mutton-chop whiskers, and he was very strict. To him, children should never be heard. We visited quite often when we lived in Newark in my early years and had to be on our best behaviour at all times, particularly when sitting at the dining table. It was very difficult to sit still on Grandpa's dining chairs, because they were stuffed with horsehair, which used to prick uncovered legs (I was in shorts in those days). I recall one event which had a lasting effect on me. The table was lit by candlelight, and I had discovered that you could put your finger through a white flame without getting burnt. Unfortunately, I continued doing it even after being told to desist by Grandpa. So he grabbed my hand and held my finger in the flame long enough to hurt but not long enough to cause much damage. I told you he was strict. Well, I certainly learned a lesson.

On the brighter side, he did have an unusual sense of humour, which I seem to have inherited. At Christmas, he excelled at charades and would have the whole family in fits of laughter, but most of the time he was very staid, as befitted his position in society. He was well known and highly regarded in the town and served as a councillor. He eventually became an alderman of Newark.

He was a tough old chap. Once when chopping logs, the axe

George and Catherine Perfect of Newark-on-Trent, my maternal grandparents

slipped and he gashed his leg quite badly, but rather than bother with a doctor, he got his wife to stitch the wound with needle and thread.

He had a large family of twelve children who survived infancy, and each child was given a name beginning with E – Egbert, Edith, Edgar, Ethelbert, Euclid and Eliza were the children from his first marriage to Elizabeth, and when she died, he married her sister Catherine. In those days it was frowned upon to marry one's late wife's sister, but it was not illegal, so the wedding went ahead. They then had six more children – Edgar, Ernest, Essie, Edric, Eustace Eiffel and Eva Eulalia, who were half-brothers and -sisters to the first lot and also cousins too. My mother was Eliza, whose mother, Elizabeth, died shortly after giving birth to her.

Whilst on the subject of my family, I am going to add a little about my elder brother, Alfred. He featured a lot in my life and, him being six years older, I looked up to him. He often helped me out when I got into scrapes, and we were always good friends. We were completely different in character, he being the steady, more serious one. We had a middle brother, James, but he was more aloof, and I didn't get on with him so well. Perhaps it was because we were closer in age – three years apart – or that he did not share our sense of humour. Alfred was fascinated by anything mechanical and liked fixing things. We all expected that he would follow Father into the clock-making world, but he ended up in the giant world of heavy engineering.

Before that, when he was sixteen, he entered a competition in a magazine called *Boy's Pictorial* and won a prize of £200 which was a fortune in those days. He used the money to set himself up with the very latest form of entertainment – *radio*.

I suppose nowadays he would be classed as a nerd or an anorak, because he kept meticulous diaries, notes and scrapbooks detailing every aspect of the very early days of radios. He recorded details of programmes, quality of sound, wavelengths used and so much more. This unique record was, many years later, after Alfred's death, donated to the Sound Archive at the British Library (near St

Pancras Station), where it featured in an exhibition at the library celebrating early days of radio. Alfred would have been very proud but at the same time highly amused to think that his "jottings" had gone to the national archive.

I cannot miss this opportunity of writing about my wife's family at this point. Her father had worked on the railways since he was a lad, and eventually became a stationmaster and signalman. He once held up the Mablethorpe train so that we could catch it. There were nine of us, me and my wife and two girls, my wife's sister with her four children. We had just been given a lift to the station by my brother-in-law (imagine ten of us in a small car) and were running a bit late. Sometimes, as a treat, he would let us go into the signal box to watch him at work. I even had a go at moving the points, but it was much harder than it looked – quite a skill. You had to wrap a cloth round the handle to prevent the friction from causing huge blisters or torn skin. The girls used to enjoy counting the wagons on the goods trains as they trundled by. Regulations were more relaxed in those days. When he lived beside the line in a railway cottage, he got to know the engine drivers very well, and they came to a mutual agreement. He would shoot a couple of rabbits, wait for the slow goods train, toss the rabbits on board the tender and the fireman would throw a large piece of anthracite into the nearby ditch, to be collected after dark. In those days, it was commonplace for country folk to exchange produce for services or other goods.

After work, he would spend hours toiling in the garden, and when he finished, he would wash under the yard pump. I don't know how he could stand such cold water on his head. He sometimes scrubbed his neck with a small brush, to get into the creases in his neck, but one day, with water in his eyes, he picked up the wrong brush, one which he had previously used to black his boots, and gave his neck a good blacking. For once the joke was on him. It took a lot of carbolic soap to clean him up afterwards.

He would sit at the head of the table in the kitchen waiting for his food, and after the main course, he would sit with his knife and fork in hand, waiting for his pudding. The only time he used a spoon was when he had a milk pudding like rice, semolina or tapioca, which wasn't often, because he preferred apple pie and custard, fruit crumble, spotted dick, jam roly-poly or treacle tart or sponge. The table at their house was always full of food, and we would sit under the bacon hanging from the ceiling, with a couple of fly papers too, in a large kitchen warmed by a big black range. They had a small scullery for washing-up and a huge pantry with marble slab for storing produce, all neatly labelled. Jars of jam, honey and numerous types of pickle (onions, cabbage, piccalilli, walnuts) would be stacked, as well as blackberry cordial, elderberry wine, rosehip syrup, sloe gin and crab apple jelly. Outside in the wash house there would be racks of apples, potatoes, turnips, etc., stored for the winter.

Chapter Seventeen
First Car – On the Road Again

When I was young, I did a lot of cycling, as it was the quickest way to get around, because we did not have a car. (Not many people were car owners in the first decades of the twentieth century – they could not afford it.)

My first bike was handed down to me by my two brothers – much used but well cared for. I learned to ride it on East Common, which was generally called "cow paddle". It was a great incentive to stay upright to avoid falling on something unpleasant, even though it would have been a soft landing. Once I was working, I progressed on to a motorbike. I like a bit of speed, as you will have discovered in a previous chapter. At one point in my life I bought a scooter, a Vespa, to travel to and from work, because it was easier to park than a car. This meant that I did not have to wait for the early and late buses after my shift.

I mentioned my first and second cars in Chapter 10. My next car was a Ford Anglia, which had only one previous owner. We were moving up the car-owning ladder very slowly. The Ford was much more stylish and modern, with an 800 or 900cc engine, which was more responsive than the battered Morris. Sometime in the 1960s I traded this car in for a *brand-new* Ford Anglia 1200, in white, with a dark green "go faster" stripe and a raked rear window. This car had synchromesh on all four gears and was great to drive, because it packed some oomph. The Anglia 1200 caused quite a stir on our camping tour of Europe, especially in Switzerland, whence it had not yet been exported. That extra engine capacity was very welcome in such a mountainous country. In every campsite where we pitched up, we soon had a crowd of men around the car wanting to look under the bonnet and asking lots of questions about performance. It would have made mincemeat of Porlock Hill!

Now for Something Completely Different…

Sport – I've never been one for playing sport, but I do like to watch on occasion, such as Saturday-afternoon wrestling, rugby and football on the TV. I once went to a football match in Leicester, in the old Filbert Street ground. It was a match between Leicester and Lincoln. However, it was an extremely foggy day, and you could see less than a quarter of the pitch, but the game went ahead. It was a strange sensation hearing the odd cheer coming from one corner of the field, from invisible people. I can't remember if the game continued or if there was any score, but it was certainly unusual. I think that today it would have been cancelled.

Cricket – My mates at work were looking for a spare bat for the local cricket team and somehow, against my better judgement, I agreed to help them out. I hadn't touched a cricket bat since I left school, but that didn't seem to bother them. The match was to be played on a Sunday in the local park. Our team won the toss and opted to bat, so I was kitted out with whites and a bat, and assured that I probably would not be called, as our opposition were no great shakes. So I sat on the end of the bench awaiting a possible call, hoping it would not come.

The innings started well, with openers putting up a good show with numerous boundaries and a six, building the score steadily. I began to relax. Big mistake. Whatever the reason, my team began a batting collapse, and in no time at all, I was called in – as last man! I strolled on to the pitch, trying to look confident, and did all the prep at the wicket – my heart was pounding. Please no quack quack! The bowler, a big chunk of a man, came thundering towards me.

Smack, I hit the ball – the shockwave from the bat nearly broke my arm again – at least that's what it felt like. I hit the ball… run! I ran like the wind and scored two. The next ball I missed, but the third ball… *owzat!* Innings over, now it was time to field. I don't know what my position was called, but I thought it was a bit too close to the batsman for comfort. The captain told us all to be alert, as we had a good chance of winning. The innings proceeded steadily, with the opposition slowly building a score, with the loss of their openers and a couple more players. It was then that their big chunky bowler took up the bat. He really was a huge fellow. He gave the ball a tremendous whack, which I'm sure you could have heard miles away. Just before the hit, my attention had wandered, so I did not see the ball heading my way. It hit me right in the solar plexus, severely winded me and doubled me over. I was helped from the field and the game continued. We managed to win the game – yes, you've guessed – by just two runs! I have never played adult cricket since.

It was just before Christmas 1951 that we acquired our first television set. It cost about £70, which was a lot of money in those days, more than a week's wage, so we paid for it monthly. It had a large cabinet which housed a huge cathode ray tube – nothing like today's slimline models. Such a bulky item needed a substantial piece of furniture to hold it, so we asked a neighbour, who was a joiner, to make us a cabinet. He produced a very neat oak cupboard and made a good living from the production of TV cabinets once the word got around.

In the early days of television, black and white, of course, there were not many programmes. There were none in the morning, and evening television finished at ten o'clock with Big Ben chimes and the National Anthem. Children's hour was at 5pm and had such programmes as *Muffin the Mule* with Annette Mills, *Bill and Ben the Flowerpot Men* and *Andy Pandy*. They were all puppet shows.

Programmes did not follow on straight away, so short films were shown to fill the gap. These were called interludes and featured such things as a boat trip down a peaceful river, a windmill turning, waves breaking on the rocks and the potter's wheel. This featured a potter raising a pot on a wheel, but it was never ever finished, because when you thought it was done, the potter would push it down and begin again. No matter which interlude it was, we watched, because it was such a novelty to us. Broadcasts would frequently break down, and then a sign would appear on the screen: "Normal service will be resumed as soon as possible." Sometimes an interlude would be shown.

If we wanted to turn the television off, we had to get off our seat and switch the set off manually – no remote control in those days! When you turned the TV on, it would take a couple of minutes to warm up. TV presenters were expected to wear evening dress and to speak with "cut glass" pronunciation – no regional accents allowed. There was also only one channel – BBC.

Programmes included *The Grove Family* (an early soap), *Educating Archie*, which transferred from radio, but not well, *Whacko*, *Dixon of Dock Green*, which was a police series shown on prime-time Saturday evening. "Ev'ning all."

A great favourite on Sunday evening was *What's My Line?* This game show, chaired by Eamonn Andrews, had a panel of four – Gilbert Harding, Lady Isobel Barnett, Marghanita Laski and David Nixon (a magician) – who had to guess the occupation of members of the public by asking questions with yes or no as the answers, and they only had a limited number of questions.

On 6th February 1952, King George VI died, and his funeral was shown on the television. The neighbours without televisions were invited in to watch and were thrilled by the pomp and ceremony. However, the following year, on 3rd June 1953, it was the coronation of Queen Elizabeth II. Once again the neighbours were invited in to watch the excellent coverage of this special day. We even had a street outing (see Chapter 6).

It was around this time that the girls started their campaign to have a pet. Were they successful? …Please turn the page.

We had very few pets over the years. The first was a canary, which we acquired not long after we moved into our new home together. We thought it would be good company for Alice, who was on her own all day. A dog would have been more company, but Alice had a fear of dogs, even though she was brought up in a house where her mother always had a dog. She was also a country girl who came into contact with lots of different types of livestock, but for some reason, she was afraid of dogs.

How about cats? Alice quite liked cats but didn't think it right to keep a cat with such a tiny garden and a main road nearby. Cats need to roam. More about cats later.

So it was the canary. All went well for a short time. It was lovely to hear its joyful singing as the sun rose each morning, but we soon discovered a problem. When I was on late shift, especially in summer, when the sun rose very early, I often didn't get home until after midnight. I'd be in a deep sleep, but I would be woken very early by the incredibly piercing warbling coming from the canary, even though we covered his cage to keep it dark – it wouldn't be fooled. I needed my sleep, so the canary was found another home.

Cats. When the girls were about five and ten years old, they kept pleading for us to have a kitten. By now we had moved to a house with a much larger garden, on a fairly quiet road. Alice and I held out against this pleading on the grounds that we often went to visit family at weekends, and we couldn't take a cat with us or ask anyone to look after it. But fate stepped in. A skinny black cat began to hang around our back door, meowing pitifully. Of course we couldn't shoo it away, so we began to feed it. It never came into the house and would vanish after being fed, but the girls loved it and the cat allowed them to stroke it. They called it Sooty. Then one day it failed to appear, and we never saw it again. I hope he found his way back to his real home.

The second cat who adopted us arrived in the same way – meowing at the back door. This cat was also black, but this one had white paws. The girls immediately wanted to adopt him, and before Alice and I could say anything, the cat jumped onto the step and went into the kitchen. He obviously adopted us. We asked around the neighbourhood if anyone had lost a black cat with white paws and put a notice in the local shop window but had no response, so Monty was here to stay. All was going well... until that fateful day!

In those days we did not have a fridge, so perishable foods like milk and cheese were kept on a marble slab in the pantry. Meat was kept in a meat safe. This was a small cupboard with a mesh front. This was also a time of continued meat rationing. One small joint of meat and perhaps a few sausages was the ration for the week. Alice had been to the butcher that Saturday morning, standing in the inevitable queue and buying a small joint of beef for Sunday. It cost eight shillings (you will have to Google how much that is in today's money), which was quite expensive, so it was looked after very carefully. Alice unwrapped it, placed it on a plate in the meat safe and closed the door. We all carried on with our Saturday chores, had lunch and the girls went off to the Saturday matinee at the local cinema. They arrived home hungry as usual and decided to feed the cat before they had their tea, but where was he?

At this time of day he was usually waiting by his bowl for food. We searched the house and garden, but there was no sign of him. We thought perhaps he had gone exploring and would be back later, so we left the back door ajar for when he returned. I went into the living room to play Ludo with the girls whilst Alice busied herself in the kitchen. We heard Alice shout, followed by a loud bang, so we rushed into the kitchen to find Alice in tears. She had evidently heard a noise in the meat safe and, thinking it may be mice, took off her slipper to whack whatever it was with. You've probably guessed – it was the cat, who had been gorging himself on our Sunday joint!

What a *cat*astrophe! Alice had not latched the meat safe door properly, leaving just enough space for a cat to get his paw in, to get his reward. The door always closed itself after use, but it needed latching by hand. The loud bang we heard? That was Alice throwing her slipper at Monty but hitting the cupboard instead. What did Monty do? He made a rapid exit via the back door. We never saw him again. We had sausages for Sunday lunch that weekend, and no cold meat and pickle on Monday, because we could not face the remains of the beef, which we took round to a neighbour for their dog rather than throw it away.

Did we have any more pets? ...No

However, there is still one animal "tail" to tell. We had a problem with mice in the house, long after the cats had gone. We tried using traps, with limited success, so then we put down poison. Nothing much happened for a while, but we had an unpleasant smell in our living room but could not trace it. One day, Alice was spring cleaning and was vacuuming everywhere. She lifted up the seat cushion on my armchair only to discover a completely flat mouse! At last we found out where the smell came from, but it was a strange feeling to think that I had flattened the poor creature. I just hope it was dead before I sat on it. After that, I feel a pun coming on.

Q. What is every cat's favourite colour?
A. Purr-ple.

Q. What is every cat's favourite quote from Shakespeare?
A. Tabby, or not tabby.

OK, I'll stop! (Until next time.)

Whilst on the subject of animals, I took the family to Loughborough to see the Boxing Day Meet of the Quorn Hunt. This was a traditional event which always drew a large crowd to the market square. There were lots of riders and a fine pack of hounds. Well, one lady rider was having difficulty getting through the crowd, and I could see that she needed a little help, so I called out in a loud voice, "Make way for a naval officer!" That did the trick: the crowd parted like the Red Sea and the young lady rode sedately through the gap, tapping her helmet with her crop as a way of thanking me. I think that my wife and girls were quite embarrassed. Another embarrassment for my wife came when we visited some friends who lived near Runnymede. George had been in the army and retired as a major, and he thought we'd like to visit the military memorial there. So, George and his wife Mary took Alice and myself on a visit. George donned his uniform for the occasion. At the end of the trip, George asked if we would like to sign the visitor book, which we did. There was a space after the signature, entitled regiment. Well, as you know, I had a reserved occupation during the war so had no regiment, but I had served in the Home Guard, so that is what I wrote – "HOME GUARD"! Alice was cross with me, and embarrassed, but luckily George and Mary saw the funny side of it. Well, we all served King and country in our own way.

Chapter Eighteen
The Bus Stops Here

In the early 1970s I began to suffer more and more with back pain. After forty years driving heavy vehicles, my back had had enough, and no amount of therapy helped, so I decided to ask to be put on light duties. This was approved, and so I ended up in the parcel office. In those days, buses would regularly transport parcels around the county where each village had an agent, which was usually in the pub or local shop.

Another reason I wanted to give up driving was the pending introduction of one-man buses, in which drivers had to dispense and check tickets. Conductors were being phased out. I thought it would be too much to cope with, and so the parcel office it was. This had the added bonus of being regular hours, plus, I still got to meet the public. I spent a couple of years in the office, and my poor back improved a great deal. Then the day came for me to retire – 7th November 1976. No more rule book, no more shifts, no more being controlled by the bell – freedom! Over forty years of driving buses; I wonder how many miles I covered? I like to think that it must have been over a million – it certainly felt like it at times. How did I stick it out for that time? I was lucky in having my lovely Alice by my side and also being blessed with two beautiful daughters.

It certainly helped to have a good sense of humour and an endless supply of cups of tea. Alice retired a few months before me, so we had lots of time to indulge in our usual hobbies such as gardening and baking, as well as beginning new hobbies like old-time dancing.

When we went dancing, I usually took my laughing tin. When an evening was slow to get started, I would turn over the laughing tin in my pocket. This made it emit a very loud, contagious laugh, which usually got the party started. If that failed, then there was a similar device in a little bag which *mooed* very loudly. Sometimes it would be the clockwork dentures on the drink tray or occasionally they were launched across the floor. As a last resort it would be a plastic fried egg on the seat. I also had a stock of long yarns with unexpected punchlines. (Don't worry, I'm not going to burden you with one at the moment.)

We went to one particular dance club dinner where the ice was taking too long to thaw, so I placed another of my secret weapons on the table next to the salt and pepper pots. It was a small tin which looked exactly like a mustard pot. Everything was fairly subdued until the main course arrived. One of the ladies decided that she would like some mustard with her beef. She reached across the table, picked up the "mustard" and started to remove the lid, when… out shot a paper snake, which startled everyone. This shock was followed by laughter all round, so a pleasant evening was had by all.

Q. Why couldn't the snake see where he was going?
A. His windscreen vipers were not working.

It was at another meal that Alice and I witnessed an incident which was embarrassing for some and funny for others. It featured a glass eye (the subject of eyeballs seems to come up quite often in my story).

Alice and I had been shopping in a local supermarket and decided to have lunch in the restaurant. I was aware of the couple at the next table, just as we were taking our coffee. They had just started to eat, when the man's glass eye fell out and landed on his dinner, staring up at him from the gravy on the plate. He immediately picked it up, wrapped it in a serviette and made his way to the gents to deal with it. His wife was looking rather upset, so I leaned over and asked if I could do anything to help. She thanked me and asked if I could take his dinner to the kitchen so that it could be kept hot. I was only too glad to oblige and explained to the chef what had happened, and he put the dinner in the hot cupboard whilst at the same time trying to hide his mirth. The man returned after about five minutes, with his glass eye in place, whereupon the chef delivered the dinner in person. (I did notice several of the staff having a bit of a smile at the poor man's expense.)

I know that in some cultures, sheep's eyes are considered a delicacy, but not one I would care to try, so I think I would find it impossible to eat my dinner with my own eye staring up at me from the plate.

Perhaps one of the following dishes might tempt me: *eyes* cream, r*eyes* pudding, fr*eyed* egg, sock*eye* salmon and so the list goes on. (I can hear you groaning!)

Back to the old-time dancing: fancy dress night was always fun; it brought out the creative side of the dancers. There were people dressed as dinosaurs, Frankenstein's monster, cowboys, Indians, Dracula and fairies, to name a few. I dressed as Santa, an Arab prince, a Zulu warrior, a Chinese mandarin and a spaceman over the years, and often wondered what reaction I would get if I was ever stopped by the police.

One year I went dressed as a vicar, complete with wig, glasses, false moustache and a collecting bag. Nobody recognised me, so, using a "vicar's voice", I went round the room collecting for charity. Some people complained that they didn't think it the right time or place for a vicar to be asking for money but had a good laugh when the culprit was revealed. They should have guessed! Anyway, I made quite a bit of money for the local hospice, so all was forgiven.

I mentioned previously that I once went to a dance dressed as Santa Claus. I used that costume on numerous occasions; for example, some old friends of ours invited us round for a pre-Christmas meal. I took my Santa suit because I knew that their grandchildren would be there too. I smuggled the suit in and waited for the right moment. The children were engrossed in a game, so I sneaked out, got dressed, picked up a sack of goodies and "ho-hoed" into the living room. The children's faces were a picture – they were so thrilled that Santa came to see them with some treats. They promised to be really good, so I told them that I would pop by on Christmas Eve – if they went to bed when Mum and Dad said. I think they really believed it was the real jolly fellow, because he knew their names. I said goodbye, and whilst they were busy opening their treats, I hurried to get changed. Everyone wanted to know where I had been because I had just missed Santa. I told them I had been to the toilet but had seen him on his way out of the back door to where his reindeer were waiting, then I had waved him off.

Alice had worked in an infant school, so in retirement, I was sometimes asked to be Santa, because none of the children knew me. (Some of the older children thought it was perhaps the caretaker dressed up, but then he would appear next to me.) I loved seeing their little smiling faces and sparkling eyes – and that was just the teachers! I think playing Santa is one of the best parts to play because you can really ham it up and at the same time spread a little happiness and joy. The only drawback was having to wear a wig, which makes one's head hot, and the awful scratchy beard. But it was all for a good cause – making children happy.

When wearing a costume, people often did not recognise me or thought I was someone else – a case of mistaken identity. I seem to have one of those faces that looks like other people. For example, in the early days of my Shetland tours, the Queen's official car was loaded onto the ferry at Aberdeen, ready for Her Majesty's visit the following week. Later, one of the crew sought me out in the bar where I was having a cup of tea and asked if I was the Queen's chauffeur. Unfortunately, I had to say no, even though I would have enjoyed taking the royal limousine for a spin. I suppose it was a case of seeing the uniform and not the person that made the crew man make the wrong choice.

Another occasion of mistaken identity involved Prince Bernhard of the Netherlands. A young naval cadet, Mike, who was the son of friends of ours, was passing out at HMS *Ganges*, the Navy training college. He was chosen to be "Button Boy" for the day. Let me explain. On passing-out day, cadets would man the rigging of the old sailing ship, and one lad would have the "honour" of climbing to the very top of the highest mast and haul himself up onto the small round platform situated there. The platform was known as the "button" – hence Button Boy. I could never have done that! Anyway, when it came to the prizegiving, the guest for the day was Prince Bernhard of the Netherlands. When Mike's name was called to receive his award, he was amazed to see who he thought was me, giving out the prizes! I suppose there was a passing likeness which had often been commented on before.

The Queen's chauffeur, Prince Bernhard, whoever next? Well, I think the time has come, for now, to apply the brakes and park up. There are many chapters still in my head, but as yet they are unwritten. So, dear reader, I hope you have enjoyed a trip on the buses, but I am afraid you will have to wait a while for the next one to come along – perhaps there may be three at once. (Only joking!)

In the meantime – keep *smiling*!